THE EVOLUTION OF FEMINIST ORGANIZATIONS

An Organizational Study

Diane Metzendorf

University Press of America,® Inc.
Lanham · Boulder · New York · Toronto · Oxford

Library of Congress Control Number: 2004116238
ISBN 0-7618-3103-7 (clothbound : alk. ppr.)
ISBN 0-7618-3104-5 (paperback : alk. ppr.)

Contents

List of Tables   iv

List of Figures   iv

Preface   v

Acknowledgements   vi

The Evolution of Feminist Organizations: An Organizational Study

Chapter 1 Introduction   1

Chapter 2 Literature Review   9

Chapter 3 Methodology   29

Chapter 4 Data Presentation   47

Chapter 5 Data Analysis   109

Chapter 6 Discussions and Implications   147

Appendix A   163

Appendix B   165

Appendix C   167

Appendix D   173

Appendix E   177

References   179

List of Tables

2.1. Comparisons of Two Ideal Types of Organizations   11

4.1 Demographics of the 15 Organizations Studied   108

5.1 Number of Discrete Job Titles   134

List of Figures

3.1. Conceptual Model   30

3.2. Eligible Organizations in Philadelphia County   38-39

3.3. Interviews with Original Organization Members   43

3.4. Interviews with Current Leaders   44

4.1. Case Study Presentation Order   48

6.1. An Empowerment Hierarchy   159

Preface

This study examines changes in feminist organizations founded in the early seventies as alternatives to traditional, bureaucratic human service organizations. Battered women's shelters, rape crisis centers and women's health and counseling centers are examples of feminist organizations linked to the Women's Movement. At inception, these organizations, reflecting feminist principles, were designed alternatively in their structure and functioning.

In-depth case studies systematically examine the life cycles of 15 feminist organizations identifying, individually and collectively, changes, over ten or more years, along the organizational dimensions of goals, authority structure, division of labor, formalization, personal relationships and rewards.

From June, 1989 to January, 1990, the research examined archival and current documentation as well as interviewed former and current organizational leaders of 15 feminist organizations in the five-county Philadelphia area. The major finding is that over time, these feminist organizations have evolved into bureaucratic structures while retaining their overarching feminist principles along certain identified dimensions.

One implication drawn from the findings is that current managers of feminist organizations do, in fact, practice feminist management which attempts to integrate their commitment to feminist principles within bureaucratic organizational structures.

Acknowledgements

Many individuals contributed to the completion of this dissertation. My Chairperson, Martha Dore, Ph.D. guided me through the process of completion with strength, wisdom and encouragement. Michael J. Austin, Ph.D. supported my efforts by advising me along the way, both as a Committee member and as my boss. Kenwyn Smith, Ph.D. stimulated my thoughts as I neared completion of the dissertation. My editor, Karlyn Messinger, encouraged me to keep on writing even when I felt like stopping.

The women who make up the feminist organizations studied in this dissertation were generous with their information and organizational materials. I sincerely appreciate their investment of time, interest and energy in this study.

Finally, my family, friends and all of my acquaintances at the various work sites I have been employed at in the last four years have been most supportive and encouraging of my doctoral efforts. In particular, my parents, Harriet and Ted Metzendorf, and my daughter, Melanie Kroungold, have been wonderful in their willingness to accept, support and encourage me in this endeavor.

Chapter 1

Alternative Organizations

The development of alternatives to bureaucratic forms of organizations has been discussed in the organizational literature (Newman, 1980; Davidson, 1980; Rothschild and Whitt, 1986 and Perlmutter, 1988). Alternative organizations have been characterized as egalitarian in the belief that they constitute the most fertile soil for the growth of nonbureaucratic forms of organizations (Newman, 1980). Growing out of this belief, alternative organizations have departed significantly from bureaucracies in goals, mode of operation, philosophy, and structure.

According to Perlmutter (1988), seven variables characterize alternative organizations: 1) commitment to social change; 2) values of equality and collegial participation in governance and policy-making; 3) new services meeting the unmet needs of a special population; 4) exploratory and/or innovative services; 5) commitment of organization personnel to the cause; 6) smallness in organizational size; and, 7) marginal economic position within the larger service system.

The early and mid-seventies were a time when many alternative organizations were founded to fill service gaps for clients whose needs were not being met by traditional organizations (Powell, 1986). Alternative organizations were frequently connected to a social movement (Sullivan, 1982).

Worker collectives are an example of alternative organizations exhibiting one or more of the characteristics identified by Perlmutter (1988). "By their own definition, they were organizations which practiced communal decision-making by allocating equal authority to every member" (Newman, 1980, p. 146). In addition, division of labor was fixed but individuals were rotated through jobs so no one became stuck in one position. Davidson (1980) defined alternative organizations in his study as organizations emerging from or in protest against traditional organizations and as reactions against existing organizational goals and structures. For instance, one alternative mental health organization studied by Davidson (1980) was started by mental health aides who left a traditional hospital setting when denied the opportunity to use their skills since they did not have appropriate degrees.

The five alternative organizations studied by Rothschild and Whitt (1986) chose not to increase the number of staff, the number of clientele, or annual budget as they aged in order to remain alternatives. In addition, they declined opportunities to receive government funding in order to maintain their alternative structures and functions.

Feminist Organizations: A Subset of Alternative Organizations

Feminist organizations are an example of alternative organizations. Feminist organizations surfaced during the early to mid-seventies and were connected to the feminist social movement. (Sullivan, 1982; Riger, 1984). At inception, feminist organizations exhibited the characteristics of alternative organizations. First, feminist organizations dealt specifically with the unmet needs of women. Victimization, lack of power, and vulnerability of women to dominant individuals and to patriarchal social, political and economic systems framed the issues addressed by feminist organizations. Battered women's shelters, multi-purpose women's centers, rape crisis centers, and health and mental health centers are examples of feminist organizations. The nature of the work in such organizations was to address issues stemming from the broader issue of women living with a patriarchal, male-dominated society. Second, feminist organizational structure addressed issues of power, domination, and oppression. Accordingly, all individual connected to a feminist organization, including clients, participated equally in delivery of services as well as in the running and policy-making of the organization (McShane & Oliver, 1978). Third, as an outgrowth of the women's movement, feminist organizations acted as vehicles for social change (Sullivan, 1982; Riger, 1984).

At inception, the major difference between feminist organizations and other alternative organizations was the emphasis placed on feminist principles to guide organizational goals, mode of operation, and program development. As opposed to other types of alternative organizations, feminist organizations were women-controlled, women-managed, and addressed the specific unmet needs of women.

Feminist Principles: A Conceptual Model For the Alternative Design of Feminist Organizations

Feminist principles are part of a belief system composed of attitudes, desires and values. The desire to be autonomous, to be valued for one's own experiences, and not to be compared disadvantageously to men compose the belief system that underlies feminist principles (Black, 1989). These belief formed the vision of the women's movement in the 1970's and drove the collective energies women invested in changing the political, social and economic systems. Black (1989) states that "success for feminists is action itself, the transforming of beliefs into action such as in organizing for women rights".

In the early and mid-seventies, feminist organizations were a vehicle for the transformation of feminist beliefs into action systems (Riger, 1984). Mirroring feminist principles, alternative organizational forms, deliberately different from the tradition forms of other human service organizations, emerged. Social services to women were provided within an organizational form that reflected the social change and empowerment principles of the feminist movement (Riger 1984).

The following feminist principles identified by Ferree and Hess (1985) guided the development of the alternative organization form for feminist organizations in the early and mid-seventies:

> The first and most basic claim of feminism is that women are a special category of people with certain characteristics in common...The second premise is that only women should define what is feminine...The third basic principle of feminism is a recognition of and dissatisfaction with living in a "man's world," where men define a "good" woman as one who meets their expectations, who serves and pleases them, who follows the rules they have created...Consequently, the fourth basic claim that feminism makes is for radical (root) change: to dismantle this "man's world," end men's unjust power, and claim for women what is rightfully theirs (p. 28).

Putting the feminist principles identified by Ferree and Hess (1985) into action, feminist organizations were consciously designed by their founders to differ from traditional human service organizations.

The Development of Feminist Organizations

It was speculated by this researcher that feminist organizations may develop differently from other alternative organizations given the unique set of principles guiding them. In 1988, this research conducted case studies of five Philadelphia feminist organizations, examining their organizational development. All were founded in the early or mid-seventies and were members of the first funding coalition for feminist organizations, Women's Way, formed in 1977. This coalition aided these feminist organizations financially to continue to provide alternative services to the women of Philadelphia. In addition, Women's Way provided group support to members of these innovative, alternative feminist organizations.

The researcher read documentation required and maintained by Women's Way for initial membership into the coalition and for yearly evaluation of each coalition members' continued compliance with Women's Way membership criteria. Included in this documentation was archival material on each organization's founding. In addition, the researcher made on-site visits to three of the five organizations and participated in interviews with executive directors.

Organizations in the pilot study were: CHOICE (Concern for Health Options Information, Care and Education); Elizabeth Blackwell Health Center for Women; OPTIONS for Women, Inc.; Women Organized Against Rape (WOAR); and Women's Law Project (WLP).

Each of these five organizations was started independently of any traditional human service organization. Their beginnings resulted from the efforts of one or more women concerned with and advocating for a feminist issue not addressed by any traditional human service organization. In fact, at inception, each of these feminist organizations was unique within its respective service area. These five feminist organizations began with a unique organizational form, very different from the bureaucratic, hierarchical form of traditional organizations. Each of the five was innovative in reflecting the participatory, egalitarian feminist ideology.

As these five organizations have evolved over time, growth has been an established pattern for each. An increase in one or more of the following dimensions has occurred for all five of the organizations: number of staff and administrators, budget, number of clients and programs. Along with growth, for each of these feminist organizations, there has been some modification in organizational form.

For example, OPTIONS for Women changed its name to OPTIONS and expanded its clientele to include men. One of the original services, job placement, was dropped. Although job placement is no longer offered, service has expanded to include staff training and community education on employment issues. While the organization still does not receive government funds, OPTIONS has broadened its funding base and market by providing consulting services to private corporations. Structurally, however, OPTIONS retains its original organizational form with co-executive directors (who are now paid) and a small staff.

Elizabeth Blackwell, CHOICE, and WOAR have experienced the greatest growth of the five feminist organizations studied. All currently have annual budgets of over $500,000. Blackwell now provides a full range of gynecological and obstetrical services. Several of their services, like the birth center, are innovative and were first within the Philadelphia health care community. In 1988, the Blackwell staff rewrote the original organizational principles in a "milder manner" (A. Schwartz, personal communication, February 21, 1989) which can, if Blackwell so chooses, broaden their funding sources and/or expand clientele. Government funding is minimal and is not accepted if it compromises the feminist principles of the organization. One feminist principle still deemed important at Blackwell is participation of employees in decision-making to the extent possible within Blackwell's current organizational structure, which is now more like a bureaucracy with management levels and specialized division of labor.

In addition to an increased budget, WOAR has experienced large program expansion, funding source expansion, and five different executive directors since its inception. As a model for other rape crisis centers throughout the United States its replication and institutionalization is extensive. A major internal reorganization occurred in 1988 which added additional managerial hierarchical levels and functional specialization to the organization's internal structure.

Program expansion has occurred for all five organizations. Programs which address current issues affecting women, such as AIDS, substance abuse, and child sexual abuse, have been and continue to be implemented.

These five feminist organizations are still woman-managed and woman-controlled, with very few men on staff. In addition, there are few males on their Board of Directors. Vertical hierarchical authority levels and horizontal specialization levels have developed along with increases in staff, although there are conscious attempts to maintain some form of participatory decision-making. Despite these efforts, egalitarian lines of authority are not present with the development of increased management levels.

Results of the Pilot Study: Implications for the Second Stage Research of This Dissertation

These preliminary case studies substantiate that, at the initial stage of development, the organizational forms of feminist organizations can be distinguished as alternative to and different from the bureaucratic forms of traditional organizations. The pilot case studies documented those differences, including: (a) the founders' personal issues and personal relationships as motivating the organizations' founding; (b) women managed and controlled organizations; (c) the presence of social change goals; (d) collective structures with consensual decision-making; and (e) extensive use of volunteer and part-time paid staff.

These preliminary case studies suggest that, over time, changes in the alternative organizational forms of feminist organizations occurred. These changes were found to be in the direction of traditional, bureaucratic organizations. Unlike the organizations studied by Rothschild and Whitt (1986) which, retained their initial alternative forms over time, the organizations in this pilot study altered their initial alternative forms with growth.

Based on these preliminary findings, a more in-depth study of the development of feminist organizations was undertaken to address the following set of questions:

1) What developmental course have feminist organizations taken, given their specific cause-oriented context?

2) What will the structure and purpose of feminist organizations look like after 10 or more years of existence?

3) How will today's feminist organizations support the feminist principles upon which they were founded?

In addition, by studying the evolution of women's organizations as organizations whose development may not fit that of traditional organizational developmental theory, there is the opportunity to identify a developmental model which more appropriately describes this subset of organizations and, perhaps, other subsets of non-traditional organizations as well.

The preliminary case studies helped to formulate a model which structured the research for this dissertation, a more extensive study of the change over time of feminist organizations. This model, in-depth case studies of the life cycles of individual feminist organizations with cross-sectional analyses at two points in time, systematically examines the evolution of feminist organizations by aggregating data along six organizational dimensions. The pilot study informed the development of four of the six dimensions in the model used to describe the unique characteristics of the alternative organizational forms of feminist organizations and to analyze changes in these dimensions over time.

One of the organizational dimensions chosen for further study is the purpose or goals of the organizations. All of the organizations in the pilot study had explicit social change goals. This is considerably different from the goals of traditional human service organizations which focus on individual change. The pilot study suggests that, over time, feminist organizations' focus on social change goals decrease as program expansion focuses on concrete services increased.

Two other dimensions identified by the preliminary research for further study were division of labor and decision-making structure. Initially, each of the five pilot organizations used a participatory, non-hierarchical model of distributing work and making decisions. Over time, however, hierarchical layers were added as well as reliance on technical specialization by organizational members. This suggests that, over time, collective structures with consensual decision-making are not maintained by feminist organizations.

The final dimension identified by the preliminary case studies for further study was personal relationships. Personal relationships were deemed crucial to the formation of feminist organizations. Working as volunteers and part-time staff enabled many women to participate in feminist organizations, not because of their expertise, but because of their personal interest in a cause or issue. A sense of togetherness developed. The pilot study indicated that, over time, although more specialization may occur, strong personal ties to feminist issues continue, as evidenced by the high level of participation of women in these organizations both as staff members and as clients.

These four dimensions, goals, structure, division of labor, and personal relationships, drawn from the pilot study, as well as two other dimensions which emerged from the literature, compose the framework for the research to be described in this dissertation, a study of change in feminist organizations over time.

Chapter 2

Literature Review

The literature review begins with a discussion of the dimensions that compose the framework used in the research for this dissertation, a study of change, over time, in feminist organizations. Illustrations from the literature on distinctions between alternative and traditional organizational forms are presented.

Next, theories of organizational development and on the transformation of social movement organizations over time are reviewed. Population ecology theory is examined in relation to environmental factors associated with changes in the organizational forms of feminist organizations. Finally, implications for further research drawn from the literature review are summarized.

A Framework for Studying Change in Feminist Organizations: The Dimensions of Organizations

Weisbord (1978) recommends six categories of organizational diagnosis: purpose, structure, relationships, rewards, leadership, and helpful mechanisms. Weisbord (1978) suggests that, by using these categories to describe and analyze organizational dimensions, a more thorough, in-depth view of the organization is obtained.

The purpose of the organization identifies the business that the organization is in. Other common names associated with the purpose of the organization are goals, missions or objectives (Weisbord, 1978).

The structure of the organization is defined by Weisbord (1978) as how the work is divided: by function, by product (program) or by both. Division of the work by function depends on the technical competence of employees and is considered to be a partner to bureaucracy. Division of the work by product or program is conducive to allowing people to do several tasks as they integrate their skills to solve a problem.

Relationships require cooperation between people as well as interpersonal skills. Relationships are diagnosed in terms of how much interdependence is required to accomplish the work and the negotiation and management of conflict among interdependent people (Weisbord, 1976).

The reward system of an organization is composed of incentives (psychological, health-related and material) that motivates and stimulate performance (Weisbord, 1978). Rewards provide employees with opportunity for growth, responsibility and achievement.

Weisbord (1978) suggest that leadership is concerned with keeping the other components of the organization in balance. Leadership requires an understanding of the organization's external and internal environment as well as keeping the organization's purpose in focus and carrying it out.

Helpful mechanisms assist in coordinating, integrating or monitoring the organization's work. One such "helpful mechanism" according to Weisbord (1978) is formalization (recorded policies, recorded procedures, agendas, meeting minutes) which help people work together.

This categorical breakdown by Weisbord (1978) supports the four dimensions identified in the pilot case studies as appropriate for a framework for the present research. In addition, several other dimensions such as leadership and helpful mechanisms are suggested. Similarly, Rothschild-Whitt (1976) uses some of the above dimensions and several others by which to compare the ideal collectivist-democratic organization to the ideal bureaucratic organization.

Descriptions of Alternative Organizational Forms

Rothschild-Whitt (1976) distinguishes collectivist-democratic organizations from bureaucratic organizations along at least eight dimensions. Table 1 contrasts these two ideal types along eight dimensions used by Rothschild-Whitt (1976). The major differences between ideal collectivist-democratic organizations and ideal bureaucratic organizations relate to difference in the dimensions of authority structure, differentiation, social relations and rewards.

Collectivist-democratic organizations are non-hierarchical, with the authority belonging to the collective, whereas bureaucracies depend on the individual's authority, based on incumbency in office and/or expertise (Rothschild-Whitt, 1976). In collective-democratic organizations, decisions are made collectively, not by individuals, and are open to negotiation. In bureaucratic organizations, there is an impersonal atmosphere with fixed rules of procedures and policies, while in collectivist-democratic organizations, personal relations are valued and expected, with few stipulated rules (Rothschild-Whitt, 1976). In addition, in the latter form, jobs are generalized; not specific nor based on technical competence or knowledge. Knowledge is shared and there is minimal division between

Dimensions		Bureaucratic Organizations		Collectivist Democratic Organizations
1. Authority	1.	Authority resides in individuals by virtue of incumbency in office and/ or experience; hierarchal organization of offices. Compliance is to universal fixed rules as these are implemented by office incumbents.	1.	Authority resides in the collectivity as a whole; delegated, if at all, only temporarily and subject to recall. Compliance is to the consensus of the collective which is always fluid and open to negotiation.
2. Rules	2.	Formalization of fixed and universalistic rules; calculability and appeal of decisions on the basis of correspondence to formal, written law.	2.	Minimal stipulated rules; primacy of ad hoc, individuated decisions; some calculability possible on the basis of knowing the substantive ethics involved in the situation.
3. Social Control	3.	Organizational behavior is subject to social control, primarily through direct supervision or standardized rules and sanctions, tertiarily through the selection of homogeneous personnel, especially at the top levels.	3.	Social controls are primarily based on personalistic or moralistic appeals and the selection of homogeneous personnel.
4. Social Relations	4.	Ideal of impersonality. Relations are to be role-based, segmented and instrumental.	4.	Ideal of community. Relations are to be wholistic, personal, of value in themselves.
5. Recruitment and Advancement	5a.	Employment based on specialized training and formal certification.	5a.	Employment based on friends, social-political values, personality attributes, and informally assessed knowledge and skills.
	5b.	Employment constitutes a career; advancement based on seniority or achievement.	5b.	Concept of career advancement not meaningful; no hierarchy of positions.
6. Incentive Structure	6.	Remunerative incentives are primary.	6.	Normative and solidarity incentives are primary; material incentives are secondary.
7. Social Stratification	7.	Isomorphic distribution of prestige, privilege, and power, i.e., differential rewards by office; hierarchy justifies inequality.	7.	Egalitarian; reward differentials, if any, are strictly limited by the collectivity.
8. Differentiation	8a.	Maximal division of labor; dichotomy between intellectual work and between administrative tasks and performance tasks.	8a.	Minimal division of labor; administration is combined with performance tasks; division between intellectual and manual work is reduced.
	8b.	Maximal specialization of jobs and functions; segmental roles, Technical expertise is exclusively held; ideal of the specialist-expert.	8b.	Generalization of jobs and functions; wholistic roles. Demystification of expertise; idea of the amateur factotum.

Rothschild-Whitt, 1976

Table 2.1. Comparisons of Two Ideal Types of Organizations

experts and non-experts, while in bureaucracies, specialization and division of labor is usual. Finally, rewards in collectivist-democrat organizations are based on friendships and are normative, as opposed to the materialistic rewards of bureaucratic organizations (Rothschild-Whitt, 1976).

The following discussion illustrates the dimensions thought to be representative of major differences between traditional and feminist organizations. The following discussion examines those significant dimensions found in the organizational literature on feminist organizations (Galper and Washburne, 1976; McShane and Oliver, 1978; Johnson 1981; Sullivan, 1982; Riger, 1984; Perlmutter, (1988).

Purpose

The purpose of an organization as reflected in its goals is found in the organization's mission statement and defines the work that the organization does (Riger, 1984). Galper and Washburne (1976) McShane and Oliver (1978), Johnson (1981), and Riger (1984) all suggest that the overall purpose of feminist organizations is to promote the welfare of women by addressing their needs through political and service activities. For example, battered women's shelters have two purposes: (1) to provide short-term escape and a supportive place for battered women; and, (2) to change the social and political conditions that foster violence against women (Sullivan, 1982). This inclusion of social change goals along with social service goals is one feature that identifies feminist organizations as different from traditional human service organizations. As Perlmutter (1988) states, "The provision of service is necessary but not sufficient" (p. 2).

Structure

A collective structure which places emphasis on democratic principles and allows for the good of the individual as well as the good of the whole by sharing power equally is one type of structure feminist organizations utilize in accordance with feminist ideology (Riger, 1984). A collective structure allows for job sharing and role rotation (Galper and Washburne, 1976) and, in the case of a battered women's shelter, enables women victims to run the shelter on an equal footing with staff and/or volunteers (Johnson, 1981). As McShane and Oliver (1978) point out:

> the structural components of alternative women's agencies generally conform to an ideological framework whose major thrust is social, economic,

and political egalitarianism (p. 618).

Leadership

The focus on egalitarianism and participatory decision-making (McShane and Oliver, 1978; Riger, 1984; Perlmutter, 1988) is the feminist organizations' attempt to distribute power equally. This concern for equal power and participatory decision-making is very different from the hierarchical authority structure of traditional bureaucracies. Individual prosperity and competition is de-emphasized, while the collective good is considered first and foremost (McShane and Oliver, 1978).

Riger (1984) suggests that certain organization dilemmas, unique to feminist organizations, result from collective structure and leaderless management. They are:

> slowness of decision-making procedures, emotional intensity, or interactions, inequitable influence processes within groups that value equality, difficult in holding member accountable, and the demands of growth (p. 105).

Relationships

In feminist organizations, relationships are emotionally intense (Riger, 1984), humanistic and personalized (McShane and Oliver, 1978). Riger (1984) states that the "level of commitment to a FMO (feminist movement organization) can by quite deep, since members may be seeking not only a work setting or a vehicle for social change, but also an experience of 'sisterhood' and 'personal acceptance' (p. 104). In this way, the organization meets the affective as well as the instrumental needs of its members.

Feminist organizations rely heavily on volunteers (McShane and Oliver, 1978; Riger, 1984) who can easily become demoralized and overwhelmed due to work overload (Valentich and Gripton, 1984). Quite different from traditional human service organizations where jobs are specialized, a member of a feminist organization any perform administrative, clerical and counseling tasks as part of her normal routine (Riger, 1984).

Reward System

The reward system of feminist organizations has been identified by

Riger (1984) as being purposive (Zald and Ash Garner, 1987). Purposive incentives (value fulfillment incentives) and solidarity (friendship) incentives are considered to be more important to members of feminist organizations (Riger, 1984) than material incentives (money and goods) (Zald and Ash Garner, 1987) which are typical motivational incentives in traditional work settings. The intrinsic reward of helping other women is emphasized (McShane and Oliver, 1978).

Equality of material rewards is a significant consideration for feminist organizations in compliance with the feminist ideology of egalitarianism and collective well being. Perlmutter (1988) describes one feminist organization's struggle to maintain an equitable pay scale between professionals and nonprofessionals whereby every other year nonprofessionals' incentives are adjusted to reflect the same median percentage as professionals'.

Formalization

Formalization, such as official recording of procedures, rules, and communications, was not a priority for feminist organizations, as nonformal methods were preferred as a means of enhancing the work setting as a collective (Riger, 1984). The nonformal group process takes its toll on efficient job performance as the focus is on the group process itself (Riger, 1984) rather than on documenting how a job was accomplished for future replication. At the initial stage of development, feminist organizations placed greater value on using the coordinating mechanisms to create a sense of collectivity and equality as opposed to more traditional concerns with formalizing coordination mechanisms to provide for future replication and work efficiency.

Summary

This literature review of the dimensions of feminist organizations at their initial stage of development distinguishes the organizational form of feminist organizations from traditional human service organizations in the following ways: (a) feminist organizations are concerned with the collective well-being of the members and consumers of the organization (McShane and Oliver, 1978) and (b) feminist organizations reflect this concern by: (1) their egalitarian, non-hierarchical, democratic organizational structure; (2) their goals (social changes and social service); (3) their participatory decision-making authority structure (McShane and

Oliver, 1978; Johnson, 1981; Sullivan, 1982; Riger, 1984; Perlmutter, 1988); (4) their rewards which are purposive (value fulfillment and friendship-based (Riger, 1984); and, (5) their nonformal methods as opposed to formalization of coordinating mechanisms (Riger, 1984).

The Organizational Development of Feminist Organizations

Feminist organizations, like other organizations, are not static; they are dynamic (Thompson, 1966) and changing. Transformations of organizations are steps in the organizational life cycle (Kimberly, 1981). With the initial stage of organizational development (birth and infancy) as the first step in the evolution of organizations, organizations transform, over time, into new forms.

A national survey of 111 shelters for battered women administered by Epstein, Russell, and Silvern (1988) explored the organizational development of one type of feminist organizations, battered women's shelters. They found that with age, shelters developed in predictable ways to which basic, widely accepted principles of organizational development were applicable (Epstein, Russell, and Silvern, 1988). Specifically, specialization and centralization of decision-making occurred along with increased role differentiation, while feminist ideology did not greatly influence structural development (Epstein, Russell, and Silvern, 1988). The researchers point out that these changes are predicted by Katz and Kahn's (1978) systems theory of specialization, which states that increased specialization and increased centralization occur along with numeric growth. According to Katz and Kahn (1978) the organization becomes more hierarchical and centralized in its decision-making process as the more specialized worker has a limited picture of the complete organization.

The next section describes the theoretical model most widely accepted in predicting changes over time in social movement organizations (Zald and Ash Garner, 19870. Feminist organizations are social movement organizations by virtue of their association with a social movement which strives to change "some elements of the social structure or reward distribution, or both, of a society" (McCarthy and Zald, 1987, p. 20). The literature on feminist organizations (McShane and Oliver, 1978, Simon, 1981; Riger, 1984) identifies feminist organizations as social movement organizations as well.

A Theoretical Model for Analyzing the Transformation of Social Movement Organizations

This theoretical approach to the organizational development of feminist organizations is based on the Weber-Michels model of transformation of social movement organizations (Zald and Ash Garner, 1987). This model is first described and then its application to analyzing research findings on the organizational development of alternative organizations, including feminist organizations, is discussed.

According to Zald and Ash Garner (1987), the institutionalization and goal displacement model of organizational transformation stemming from Weber (Gerth and Mills, 1946) and Michels (1949) is the dominant sociological approach in analyzing the organizational development of social movement organizations. This model predicts that when social movement organizations attain an economic and social base in society, and as the original charismatic leadership is replaced, a bureaucratic structure emerges, and a general accommodation to the society occurs.

Three changes occur according to this model "…goal transformation, a shift to organizational maintenance, and oligarchization" (Zald and Ash Garner, 1987, p. 121). Goal transformation usually involves the diffusion of goals so that original goals that are not attainable are replaced with goals that expand the original target population.

However, according to the Weber-Michels model, whatever the form, of goal transformation, it is always in the direction of greater conservatism (the accommodation of organization goals to the dominant societal consensus). Organization maintenance is a special form of goal transformation in which the primary activity of the organization becomes the maintenance of membership, funds, and other requirements of organizational existence. It, too, is accompanied by conservatism for the original goals must be accommodated to societal norms in order to avoid conflicts that could threaten the organization's viability.

Oligarchization may be defined as the concentration of power, in the Weberian sense, in the hands of a minority of the organization's members. (For our purposed, bureaucratization is that form of oligarchization that stresses a hierarchy of offices and prescribed rules for conduction affairs)…but the Michels part of the model treats mainly of the movement from democratic decision structures – a situation of dispersed power-moves to centralization and oligarchy (Zald and Ash Garner, 1987, p. 122).

It is the contention of Zald and Ash Garner (1987) that this model is incomplete as a statement on the transformation of social movement organizations due to its contention that transformation is always accompanied by conservatism.

The Application of the Weber-Michels Model to Analyzing the Transformation Of Social Movement Organizations

Applying the Weber-Michels model, three different authors (Newman, 1980; Davidson, 1980; Simon, 1981, 1982) analyzed organizations along the dimensions of goals, structure, and decision-making processes to determine of organizations moved in the direction predicted.

In a case study of an organization's development within the women's movement, Simon (1981) applied the Weber-Michels model of organizational transformation to an urban rape crisis center where she carried out a 10-month participant observation study.

Simon (1982) found that the feminist organizations she studied did not follow the Weber-Michels model.

Two of the three predictions of the Weber-Michels' paradigm do not apply to the subject of my 10-month study. Goal transformation did not occur. The original goals...remain central...goal expansion, did take place. New social change goals have been added to the organization's 1972 conceptions of its purpose. For example, work with child sexual abuse has become a major new dimension of the organization...goals concerning organizational maintenance have also been added to original aims...the third prediction, the Weber-Michels' prophecy concerning oligarchization, does apply to the STOP example, yet in a much more ambiguous fashion than their projection suggests...the crux of the organization's current decision-making dilemma is the challenge of preventing oligarchical build-up without inhibiting effective staff leadership (Simon, 1982, p. 489).

Simon (1982) concludes, based on her 10-month participant observation study of STOP, that for the organization to be effective as a social change agent, institutionalization is a necessary ingredient as long as the organizational leadership maintains egalitarian and democratic principles.

In her ethnographic history of twelve worker-collective organizations, Newman (1980) describes how 10 of the 12 collectives followed the predictions of Weber-Michels model. Newman (1980) found that, at the outset, these organizations did closely approximate their idealized view of an egalitarian distribution of authority, but that the process of bureaucratization began at the point that the collectives sought outside financial support. Only two of the collectives (business collectives) were able to remain structurally the same due to their ability to invest their own money in the business. Newman (1980) found that the other 10 collectives (business, service, and information) at first capitulated to the demands of funding agencies only superficially and retained their structural mechanisms for egalitarian decision-making. However, two factors led to the entrenchment of bureaucratic structures: (1) the dependence of the collective members on outside funding for their livelihood; and, (2) the addition of new volunteers which introduced structural differences between these volunteers and full-time staff.

Newman (1980) argues that:

> The bureaucratization of the collectives cannot be attributed to difficulties in the management of tasks...in short, the ethnographic histories of these 12 collectives indicate that it was not the shortcomings of collective decision-making that led to the development of bureaucratic forms of administration. Rather, it was the increasing dependence on financial support from the outside, the limited amount of that support, and the internal ramifications of funding limitations that encouraged the formation of anti-egalitarian forms of authority" (p. 160).

Davidson (1980) studied eight alternative counterculture organizations for a period of up to two years to determine if these organizations followed what he calls, "the incessant trend toward bureaucracy" (p. 165). It is Davidson's (1980) conclusion that:

> The problems of growth, hierarchy, specialization, impersonality, and technical competence were not black-and-white issues; however, they were problems of degree. While organization members varied in their tolerance for bureaucracy, they resisted these structural features when they reach a subjective point – a point where the organization began to look and feel like a traditional organization (p. 171).

These three analyses of organizational transformation of social movement organizations using the Weber-Michels model support the statement that social movement organizations do move in the direction predicted by the Weber-Michels model, although movement occurs at different rates and in varying degrees toward goal displacement (Simon, 1982) and oligarchization in the form of bureaucratization (Newman, 1980; Davidson, 1980). However, the extent to which transformation of feminist organizations to institutionalization is associated with conservatism is challenged by Simon (1982).

Summary

All three authors give examples to challenge the association of conservatism with change, for, even as these organizations have transformed, they have retained some resemblance to their original organizational form. Newman (1980) described the collectives as:

> having metamorphosed into bureaucratic institutions, stratified and fundamentally (though not explicitly) nonegalitarian. Of course, they were not constituted along the same lines as the traditional bureaucracy, with pyramid-shaped authority structures. The bureaucracy of the ten collectives tended to be two-tiered (Newman, 1980, p. 259).

Simon (1982) suggests that:

> the presence of radical and feminist ideology serves to require frequent reexamination of a structure, leadership and the quality or organizational life in the light of original group and movement values and goals (p. 499).

Davidson (1980) states that these organizations relied on:

> community days, potluck dinners, and other techniques to maintain their task/community balance (p. 175).

Population Ecology Theory

The organizational development of feminist organizations is also influenced by the external environment as well as by changing internal conditions (Zald and Ash Garner, 1987). Changes in organizational dimensions very according to the affects of environmental factors on each dimension (Zald and Ash Garner, 1987).

The following discussion focuses on population ecology theory to explain variations in the organizational forms of social movement organizations, in particular, of feminist organizations, and the retention of characteristics of the original organizational forms which are counter to conservatism, as predicted by the Weber-Michels model.

Evolutionary ecological organizational theorists (Freeman, 1982; Freeman and Hannan, 1983; Hannan and Freeman, 1984; Singh, House and Tucker, 1986) argue that change in the organizational forms of populations of organizations occur, not as a planned adaptation to environmental conditions, but as the result of an environmental selection process.

Selection refers to the external pressures exerting influence on organizations and posing contingencies resulting in population differentiation (Aldrich and Mueller, 1982, p. 39).

A selection model is used here to explain the environment as a force in the selection of organizational forms in feminist organizations.

Ecological theory (Freeman, 1982) suggests that all organizations must conform to the demands of the environment in order to survive. Organizations can take a variety of structures and forms initially, but the force of the environment will push them toward the "mean", the form most supported by the demands of the environment.

Freeman (1982) states, however, that structural inertia limits the capacity of the organizations to make radical changes in strategy and structure. Each time an environment changes, the survival chances characterizing each population also changes. What occurs, according to Freeman (1982), is that structural inertia affects population of organizations by slowing down the rate of change and increasing variation in organizational form as growth occurs at different rates. Freeman (1982) states:

We expect to find diversity of organizational forms, then, either because growth leads to change of form (metamorphic development) or because single organizations have difficulty growing fast enough and simultaneously being efficient enough to prevent the appearance of competing forms of organizations" (p. 23).

Environmental Variables Influencing the Transformation of the Organizational Form of Social Movement Organizations

Zald and Ash Garner (1987) support ecological theory by arguing that social movement transformation is conditioned or determined by environmental factors. They contend that environmental factors affect the transformation of movement organizations. The direction in which environmental factors influence social movement organizations in relation to the goals and structure of the organizations varies depending upon the type of organization and the conditions under which alternatives to the conservatizing and oligarchizing process are possible (Zald and Ash Garner, 1987). Their results in population differentiation (Aldrich and Mueller,

1982).

This is illustrated by Newman's (1980) ethnographic histories of 12 worker collectives. She found that collectives dependent upon outside funding sources moved toward bureaucratic structures, while those that maintained their own source of funding remained collective and egalitarian. Similarly, Davidson (1980) identified funding as a critical issue for the collectives he studied.

> Organizational activity fluctuated greatly as the availability of funding changed, and even when support was obtained, it usually came at a cost of purity of activities or conscience (p. 173).

Environmental Variables Influencing the Transformation Of Feminist Organizations

Availability of Funding Resources

One external factor influencing the organizational form of feminist organizations in the direction of conservatism and oligarchization is the need for finding funding resources (McShane and Oliver, 1978; Johnson, 1981; Sullivan, 1982; Riger, 1984). Riger states that:

> the transformation of goals in a conservative direction is closely linked to the availability of resources with which to sustain the organization (p. 108).

Sullivan (1982) cites battered women's shelters

> twisting themselves into pretzels to change the focus of their work to match the requirements of funding agencies and losing self-direction in the process...battered women's groups often find it difficult to define the propriety of a nontraditional model to funding and social service agencies (p. 45).

Johnson (1981) states that:

> most of the conflict between social control hierarchies and feminist ideology is rhetorical, as most shelters (including most feminist ones) have been co-opted by official social control agencies, an unintended consequence of accepting financial support from official resources (p. 828).

McShane and Oliver (1978) suggest that a feminist organization reach a crossroad in its survival changes when it decides to accept funding from within the male system. Simon (1981) suggests a multiple source funding strategy:

> for minimizing external control of a social movement organization and for reducing the probabilities of co-optation (p. 493)

In those feminist organizations which chose to obtain funding solely from within the female system, McShane and Oliver (1978) found maintenance of original goals, objectives, and feminist ideology.

Interorganizational Relationships

Another environmental factor influencing feminist organizations in the direction of the Weber-Michel model is interorganizational relationships. Interorganizational relationships include relationships with other feminist organizations offering similar services as well as relationships with traditional human service organizations with which feminist organizations must interact. Competition for consumers and resources, including large grants, is a factor influencing feminist organizations in the direction of efficiency (Sullivan, 1982). Movement in the direction of conservatizing the goals of feminist organizations comes from pressure from other social service organizations to "conform to the therapeutic, psychological orientation of most social service agencies" (Sullivan, 1982, p. 46). This becomes necessary in order to receive referrals from other organizations. A result of social control of feminist organizations by outside agencies, feminist organizational goals can be compromised. Johnson (1981) and Sullivan (1982) document the occurrence of social control phenomena on the part of the criminal justice system with battered women's shelters.

Galper and Washburne (1976) describe a feminist organization whose goal was to educate other social service organizations about its goals by providing staff training sessions. Galper and Washburne (1976) considered these efforts successful in increasing public awareness and support for the feminist organization in the form of increased referrals as well as developing a coalition of feminist therapists composed of women from both traditional and alternative settings.

Internal Variables Influencing the Transformation of the Organizational Form of Social Movement Organizations

Zald and Ash Garner (1987) state that:

> external events are not the only causes of change. Emerging bureaucratic structures, internal ideological factions, leadership styles, and other, essentially internal factors also cause organizational transformation (p. 133).

Examples of internal variables influencing changes in the organizational form following the Weber-Michels model are found in Newman's (1980) and Davidson's (1980) descriptions of alternative movement organizations.

Both Newman (1980) and Davidson (1980) cite growth, in the form of increased numbers of staff, as a factor, which moves collective organizations toward bureaucratic structure. Newman states:

> structural differences between these volunteers and the full-time staff emerged very gradually, but eventually succeeded in undermining the egalitarian process of decision-making that had obtained prior to the development of external financial dependencies (p. 154).

Also contained in this phenomenon is the division of responsibilities based on the infusion of professionalism. Davidson (1980) states:

> with expansion would come specialized positions for directors, fund-raisers and others who could attempt some control over the environment (p. 171).

Professionalism

The employment of professionals by feminist organizations leads to stratification of the organization's members. Previous to the infiltration of professionals, the existence of stratified positions was nonexistent (Riger, 1984). Simon (1982) states:

> "the danger that accompanies institutionalism is that internal 'experts' might capture and control organizational leadership" (p. 499).

Leadership

Simon (1982) feels that the emergence of leadership in feminist organizations is inevitable. Simon (1982) states that:

> organizations, which do not designate formal structures, are ruled necessarily by informal structures based on friendship network. (p. 496).

Ruling friendship networks or cliques creates divisions among members of the organization and slows down the tasks at hand. Power in decision-making stands in opposition to the democratic decision-making process to which feminist organizations are committed.

In their descriptions of two feminist organizations, both Simon (1982) and Perlmutter (1988) refer to systems of checks and balances put in place by the members of each organization to assure the continuation of democratic decision-making processes in spite of formalized leadership. Simon (1982) notes that:

> institutionalization replaces rule by informal cliques with rule by elected and formally appointed leaders. Formal leadership brings with it the potential of accountability, and, therefore, the potential of democracy. In contrast, informal rules preclude accountability and ensure tyranny (p. 501).

Perlmutter (1988) identifies several leadership characteristics essential to maintaining the egalitarian, democratic decision-making process. They are the leader's personal commitment to the ideology, capacity for risk-taking and flexibility and comfort with difference (Perlmutter, 1988). Perlmutter (1988) feels that charismatic leadership may be dysfunctional in the development of feminist organizations as it may dissuade or discourage other participants from remaining actively involved. The possibility of factions developing and more radical directions than the current direction of the leadership is cited by Simon (1982), with the eventual resignation of the director of the feminist organization.

Ideology

Social change is at the root of the ideology of feminist organizations (Riger, 1984). Social change goals guide feminist organizations in their development, shaping policies, administration, and services (Valentine and Gripton, 1984). When a feminist organization shifts from the emphasizing social change goals to emphasizing social service goals, then the organization moves toward a more conservative stance (Valentinch and Gripton, 1984).

This phenomenon is described by Murray (1988) in her article, "The Unhappy Marriage of Theory and Practice: An Analysis of a Battered Women's Shelter." She states:

> over time, many of these shelters underwent a process of transformation, from organizations supported by a feminist analysis of violence against women and a self-help practice to organizations characterized by a more narrow individualized analysis of the causes of violence and a 'professional' practice" (p. 77).

In one woman's battered shelter, she describes a gap between theory and practice, where the realities of the clients' day-to-day problems take precedence over the social change goals of empowerment and the "creation of lives free of violence and all forms of oppression". (p.79).

Simon (1982) suggests that the feminist organization's commitment to its ideology is the factor that keeps it from associating conservatism with the process of institutionalization by safeguarding the maintenance of a democratic and egalitarian process in the organization's everyday life. However, Collins and Whalen (1989) feel that:

> an assessment of the current rape crisis movement provokes concern that the increasingly institutional and professional nature of rape crisis services may lessen rather then expand social change efforts (p. 62).

Collins and Whelan (1989) suggests a rearticulation of the broad social change goals in the development of strategies that further them for social workers within rape crisis centers.

Summary

The literature cited above clearly identifies the external variables of relationships with funding sources and interorganizational relationships as influencing goal transformation and organizational maintenance of feminist organizations in the direction predicted by the Weber-Michels model. The internal variables of professionalism, leadership, and degree of ideological commitment also reflect the degree of movement of internal structures of feminist organizations toward bureaucratization. The extent to which movement in the direction predicted by the Weber-Michels model occurs (conservatism, organizational maintenance and oligarchization) depends, in part, upon the degree of influence each variable has on the feminist organization.

Implications of the Literature Review Framework for the Study

The literature review identifies those organizational dimensions which, at their initial stage of development, are considerably different from those dimensions in traditional, bureaucratic organizations. Those dimensions identified in the literature review as well as in the pilot study described earlier as different from an alternative to traditional bureaucratic organizational forms at the initial stage of development are: organizational structure, relationships, division of labor, and purpose/goals. Additionally, the literature review identified the dimensions of rewards and formalization as additional indicators of difference between feminist and traditional organizations at their initial stage of development.

The literature discusses a life cycle model (Kimberly, 1981) which places organizational change in a life cycle perspective of an organization transforming from its initial stage of development at birth and infancy to its current organizational form over time. The research undertaken here uses this life cycle perspective as a framework within which to study the changes in feminist organizations over time. By using a life cycle model, the researcher obtains a wholistic view of the organization and the transactional relationships among environmental factors which result in changes in the organizational dimensions identified in the literature review.

Theoretical Model

Theories of organizational development (Katz and Kahn, 1978; Zald and Ash Garner, 1987) and population ecology theory, in addition to the results of the pilot study, suggest that feminist organizations change over time in predictable ways along the dimensions identified. These theories (Katz and Kahn's systems' theory of specialization; Zald and Ash Garner's social movement theory; population ecology theory), as well as the findings of the pilot study, suggests that, over time, the organizational forms of feminist organizations change to resemble traditional, bureaucratic organizations. Population ecology theory suggests that retention over time of some aspects of the original organizational forms of feminist organizations is possible. The research described here provides a descriptive analysis of the changes over time in the organizational forms of a sample of feminist organizations. It seeks to determine whether feminist organizations conform to theoretical models of organizational change as indicated in the literature reviewed here.

Transactional Relationships

In addition, this dissertation explores the changes in external (funding resources and interorganizational relationships) and internal factors (growth and leadership changes) associated with organizational change over time of feminist organizations.

Conclusion

In Chapter Three information obtained from the literature review and findings of the preliminary case studies are used to develop the descriptive variables which compose the research questions guiding the study.

Chapter 3

Methodology

Introduction: The Conceptual Model

The conceptual model presented in Figure 1 is composed of the variables by which changes in the feminist organizations over time are described in this research study. The conceptual model illustrates the circularity of the interaction of the descriptive variables.

These variables, drawn from the literature review (Galper and Washburne, 1976; McShane and Oliver, 1978; Johnson, 1981; Weisbord, 1978; Newman, 1980; Davidson, 1980; Sullivan, 1982; Riger, 1984; Epstein, Russell, and Silvern, 1988) and from the pilot study, are used to describe the alternative forms of feminist organizations and the environmental factors associated with change in the feminist organizations over time. These variables comprise the focus of the research questions.

Descriptive Variables

1. Goals

Goals are the general purposes of an organization as put forth in its charter, annual reports, public statements by key executives, and other authoritative pronouncements (Hall, 1972). For purposes of this research, social change goals are those written goals of an organization that address promotion of the welfare of women through social and political activities (Riger, 1984). Client service goals are those written goals of an organization that address promotion of the welfare of women through client service activities (Riger, 1984).

Emphasis on social change goals over a client service goals at the initial stage of development in feminist organizations is well-documented in the literature (Galper and Washburne, 1976; McShane and Oliver, 1978; Johnson, 1981; Riger, 1984). The five feminist organizations in the pilot study also emphasized social change goals in their documents of incorporation.

2. Formalization

Formalization is the extent to which rules, procedures, instructions, and communications are written and distributed to everyone in an organi-

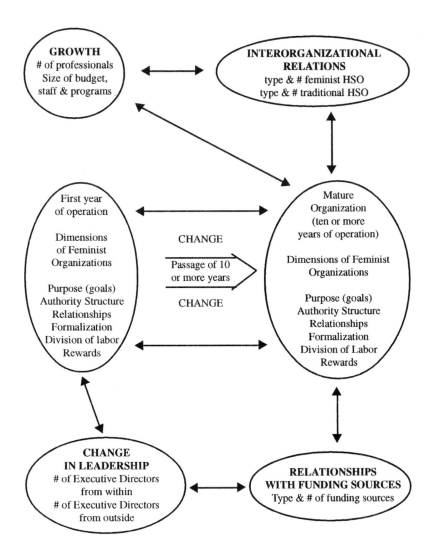

Figure 3.1 Conceptual Model

zation (Pugh, et all., 1986, p. 79).

This variable was drawn from the literature with documented that, at the initial stage of development, feminist organizations paid little attention to formalize procedures or rules (Riger, 1984). Ad hoc decision-making with few written rules is characteristic of Collectivist-democratic organizations like feminist organizations (Rothschild-Whitt, 1976).

3. Personal Relationships

The variable personal relationships is the extent to which relationships between people are effective, and of value in themselves (Rothschild-Whitt, 1976). Personal relationships are the opposite of the impersonality found in bureaucratic organizations and personality is defined as the extent to which both the organizational members and outsiders are treated without regard to individual qualities (Hall, 1963).

This variable was drawn from the literature (McShane and Oliver, 1978; Riger, 1984; Valentich and Gripton, 1984) as well as from the pilot study. Two of the feminist organizations in the pilot study were organized by women whose personal relationships led to the establishment of their organizations.

4. Reward System

Reward System includes pay differentials and other types of incentives important to the members of the organization (Rothschild-Whitt, 1976).

This variable was identified in the literature. For example, (Riger 1984) suggests that the reward system of feminist organizations was initially composed of purposive (value fulfillment), solidary, and friendship incentives. Material incentives may have been present but were not the primary motivation for participation in the organization (Rothschild-Whitt, 1976).

5. Division of Labor

Division of labor is the extent to which work tasks are subdivided by functional specialization in the organization (Hall, 1963).

This variable was drawn from the literature as well as from the pilot study. The literature documented that, at their initial stage of development, feminist organizations often had limited numbers of specialized job positions requiring technical qualifications. Work was usually distributed based on personal interest in the needs of organization (Riger, 1984). This was also the norm for the five feminist organizations in the pilot study.

6. Authority Structure

Authority structure is the existence of a hierarchy of authority, the extent to which the locus of decision making is structured by the organization (Hall, 1963).

This variable was drawn from the literature as well as from the pilot study. According to the literature, feminist organizations operated collectively with a concern for distributing power equally (McShane and Oliver, 1978). Similarly, one of the five organizations in the pilot study utilized a collective decision-making process in which all members had a voice in decision-making.

7. Funding Source

Funding source indicates where the organization receives its resources for operation and perpetuation.

This variable was drawn from the literature. The availability of funding is a crucial factor affecting the survival of feminist organizations (Riger, 1984). In order to survive, feminist organizations often expand their search for resources to include relationships with external funding sources with "strings" attached to these relationships (Sullivan, 1982; Simon, 1982; Riger, 1984). Newman (1980) found in her study that in order for the alternative organizations to survive, acceptance of outside funding becomes necessary.

8. Interorganizational Relationships

Interorganizational relationships indicate the extent to which feminist organizations compete with other feminist or traditional organizations for the same clients and funding sources and the extent to which feminist organizations receive clients from and refer clients to feminist and traditional organizations.

9. Organizational Growth

Organizational growth is defined by the number of full-time and part-time paid staff, size of the annual budget, and program expansion.

This variable was drawn from the pilot study in which growth was documented in the five organizations study. Each of the five feminist organizations studied experienced growth in one or more of the following areas: number of paid staff, annual budget, and programs.

10. Leadership

Leadership is defined as the existence of an individual or individuals in the foremost role of authority or influence in the organization.

This variable was drawn from the literature which documented leadership as a necessary ingredient for the continued survival of feminist organizations (Simon, 1982; Perlmutter, 1988).

The Research Questions

Organizational theorists Katz and Kahn (1978) and Zald and Ash Garner (1987) propose that, over time, alternative organizations change to resemble traditional, bureaucratic organizations. The research questions explore the hypothesis suggested by this literature and by the pilot study finding that the alternative forms of feminist organizations changed over time.

The research questions focus on changes, over time, in the variables described previously which were selected according to their ability to capture the differences between alternative feminist and traditional bureaucratic organizations:

1. At the tenth or subsequent year of operation of feminist organizations, have the majority of goals of feminist organizations changed from those emphasizing social change to those emphasizing client service? This research question grew out of the suggestion in the literature that, over time, the goal emphasis shifts from social change goals to client service goals (Riger, 1984).

2. At the tenth or subsequent year of operation of feminist organizations to what extent has the alternative (collective, egalitarian) organizational structure of feminist organizations changed to a hierarchical, bureaucratic structure?

This research question crew of the observations in the literature (Newman, 1980; Davidson, 1980; Epstein, Russell, and Silvern, 1988) as well as findings of the pilot study that, over time, alternative structures become hierarchical.

3. At the tenth or subsequent years of operation in feminist organizations, have jobs become specialized? This research question grew out of the observations in the literature (Epstein, Russell, and Silvern, 1988) suggesting that the level of job specialization increased with the organization's age.

4. At the tenth or subsequent year of operation of feminist organizations, how does the degree of formalization differ from that found in the first year of operation of feminist organizations?

This research question grew out of the suggestion in the literature (Riger, 1984) and the pilot study that, as feminist organizations age, formalization of rules and procedures increases.

5. In the tenth and subsequent year of operation of feminist organizations, has the emphasis on purposive rewards and rewards of friendship shifted to an emphasis on material rewards?

This research question grew out of the observations in the literature (Galper and Washburne, 1976) that, over time, material rewards become more important to organization members as the gap between their salaries and those of colleagues in established agencies is noted (Galper and Washburne, 1976). Differential pay is another indicator of job specialization over time (Katz and Kahn, 1978).

6. In the tenth or subsequent year of operation of feminist organizations, has the emphasis on personal relationships shifted to an emphasis on impersonality?

The literature suggest that, over time, professionalism increases as documented in the case studies on alternative organizations (Newman, 1980) and in a case study on a battered women's shelter (Murray, 1988).

7. At the tenth or subsequent year of operation of feminist organizations, how has the interaction between the external and internal environmental factors (relationships with funding sources, interorganizational relationships, leadership changes and organizational growth) and feminist organizations changed?

This research question is drawn from population ecology theory which suggests that, as the environment changes, organizations will move closer to the norm. This occurred in the case of the alternative organizations (Newman 1980) studied when these organizations increased their dependence on outside funding sources for monies.

Design

The exploratory nature of the questions that underlie this study suggests a non-experimental, naturalistic design (Reid and Smith, 1981. The descriptive nature of non-experimental research is compatible with the purpose of this research which is to identify how the dimensions of feminist organizations have changed 10 or more years since their inception. The descriptive non-experimental design " breaks wholes down into interconnected parts, to achieve as detailed a picture as possible" (Reid and Smith, 1981, p. 70. Although this type of research does not explain cause-effect relationships between variables, it can give information about the presence of associations among factors (Reid and Smith, 1981). Because the non-experimental design does not control or manipulate the independent variables(s), the researcher cannot conclude cause and effect (Reid and Smith, 1981). However, it does allow the researcher to provide information about characteristics of the phenomenon studied (Reid and Smith, 1981).

Non-experimental designs have been employed in research on social movement organizations (Newman, 1980; Davidson, 1980) and research on feminist organizations (Simon, 1981; Hooyman and Cunningham, 1986 Epstein, Russell, and Silvern, 1988).

Non-experimental designs are compatible with research on populations of organizations after the passage of time (Kimberly, 1976; Kimberly, 1980; Singh, House, and Tucker, 1986). By using a non-experimental design, the researcher does not intrude upon nor alter events which occur naturally as time passes in the organizations' lives. Events are not influenced by the researcher, as in the case of experimental design. The events would have taken place naturally (Reid and Smith, 1981) without manipulation by the researcher.

The design that is best suited to study the development of organizations over time is the longitudinal design (Kimberly, 1976). As opposed to the cross-sectional design which is based on data collected at a single point in time, the longitudinal design supports a process-oriented approach (Kimberly, 1976).

> Either implicitly or explicitly, the questions focus on the interaction among variables in a setting which unfolds in social time (Kimberly, 1976 page 225).

Points out that longitudinal research can facilitate the development of better models of growth and change in the study of organizations. This further supports the use of a longitudinal research designed to examine the life cycle of feminist organizations.

Sampling

A non-probability purposive sample was obtained. Purposive samples:

> Consists of elements (respondents, cases, time segments, and so on), deliberately chosen or handpicked for the study's purposes (Reid and Smith, 1981, p. 173).

In this study, the sample was drawn from the specific geographical area. In addition, only organizations defined as mature, those in existence for 10 or more years, were chosen. Although purposive sample limits the ability to generalize to the larger population, it allows the researcher to study a specific population more closely, as in the present study.

Sample Selection

Names of feminist organizations in Philadelphia, Delaware, Bucks, Chester and Montgomery counties were obtained from variety of sources: Women's Way, the Mayor's Commission on Women of the City of Philadelphia, the Community Services Planning Council "Where to Turn Directory," "Women's Yellow Pages," and United Way of Southeastern Pennsylvania Directory. Initial telephone calls were made by the researcher to determine eligibility of the organization based on the following criteria: (a) incorporation by majority of women 10 or more years ago; and (b) an avowed organizational purpose at inception of providing services to women.

Each organization was sent a letter of introduction (Appendix Z) and then contacted by telephone by the researcher to determine its willingness to participate in the study. The letter of introduction introduced the researcher, explained the purpose of this research study, and requested the agreement of the organization's representatives (either the Board President or the Executive Director) to participate in the study. In addition, an "Agreement to Cooperate in Study" form (Appendix B) accompanied the introduction letter. On this form, the organization's representative had the opportunity to articulate the organization's expectations of the researcher to uphold client and organizational confidentiality. Both the organization's representatives and the researcher signed this form at the time of the researcher's visit to the organization.

Philadelphia County had 11 eligible feminist organizations. Each of the four other counties had four or fewer feminist organizations eligible to participate in this study. A random sampling of the 11 eligible Philadelphia County feminist organizations was carried out in which five feminist organizations were selected to participate in the study. These five Philadelphia feminist organizations were selected by a) the sampling process presented in Figure 2, described below; and, b) their willingness to participate in the study. If all of 11 eligible Philadelphia feminist organizations had been included in this study, over-representation of the feminist organizations in Philadelphia County would have occurred.

The selection criteria for Philadelphia County organizations consisted of a) alphabetizing the names of the eligible organizations; and b) choosing every other organization. Alphabetical random sampling assured that every organization was given equal chance to be selected for participation in this study as no order was assigned (Kalton, 1987). Three of the organizations selected declined participation. One organization was concerned with confidentiality issues which prohibited it from participating. The other two organizations declined due to lack of time. The organizations that appeared next on the list replace the organizations that declined to participate in the study.

The five organizations that participated are: Interim House, Philadelphia Women's Network, Women in Transition, Women Organized Against Rape, and The Women's Therapy Center. Figure 2 illustrates the sampling process for Philadelphia County as well as the organizations' willingness to participate in the study.

In Bucks County, there were three eligible feminist organizations. One chose not to participate in this study, due to lack of time on the part of key personnel. The two that did participate are A Woman's Place and Women for Sobriety.

In Chester County, there were three eligible feminist organizations. One chose not to participate in the study, due to lack of time. The two that participated in the study are Crime Victims' Center of Chester County and the Women Suburban Clinic.

In Delaware County, there were four eligible feminist organizations. One of the organizations chose not to participate in the study, due to staffing problems. The three that participated are Domestic Abuse Project, Women Against Rape and the Women's Resource Center.

In Montgomery County, there were three eligible feminist organizations. All participated in the study. They are the Birth Center, the Women's Center of Montgomery County, and the Victims Service Center.

Figure 3 identifies the sampling of the four counties by the type of each organization asked to participate in the study, those organizations that refused and the reasons why they refused, and those organizations that participated in the study.

Summary

A total of 15 organizations were selected to participate in this study. The sample of 15 feminist organizations is considered to be representative of all eligible feminist organizations in the five county area. The 15 feminist organizations selected represent the major issues for which women's organizations were established, as identified in the literature. Organizations addressing these issues of rape, domestic violence, women's

Organization Name	Type of Organization	Participation or Refusal and Why
CHOICE	Health Information and Referral	Not selected
+Elizabeth Blackwell Health Center	Health Care	Refused, no time
* Interim House	Substance Abuse	Participated
OPTIONS	Career/Employment	Not Selected
* Philadelphia Women's Network	Career/Employment	Participated
+Women Against Abuse	Domestic Violence	Refused. Confidentiality
+Women in Transition	Multi-Service	Participated
* Women Organized Against Rape	Rape	Participated
+Women's Alliance for Job Equity	Career/Employment	Refused, no time
Women's Law Center	Legal	Not Selected
* Women's Therapy Center	Mental Health	Participated

* Organizations included in the final sample
+Organizations that were sampled but refused participation

Figure 3.2. Eligible Organizations in Philadelphia County

Organization Name	Type of Organization	Participation or Refusal and Why
BUCKS COUNTY		
* A Woman's Place	Domestic Violence	Participated
+Network of Victims Assoc.	Comprehensive Victims' Center	Refused, no time on part of key personnel
* Women for Sobriety	Substance Abuse	Participated
CHESTER COUNTY		
* Crime Victims' Center	Comprehensive Victims' Center	Participated
+Domestic Violence Center	Domestic Violence	Refused, no time of key personnel
* Women's Suburban Clinic	Health	Participated
DELAWARE		
* Domestic Abuse Project	Domestic Violence	Participated
* Women Against Rape	Rape Center	Participated
+Women's Association for Women's Alternatives	Career/Employment	Refused, no time staff shortage
* Women's Resource Center	Information and Referral	Participated
MONTGOMERY COUNTY		
* The Birth Center	Health	Participated
* Victim Services Center	Comprehensive Victims' Center	Participated
* Women's Center of Montgomery County	Domestic Violence	Participated

* Organizations included in the final sample
+Organizations that were sampled but refused participation

Figure 3.2. Eligible Organizations

health care, career/employment, and substance abuse, are represented in the study sample. This sample represents hotlines, counseling services, and shelters.

Methodology

This exploratory study utilized qualitative data obtained from archival and current organization documents and interviews with original organization members and current leaders. This methodology allowed the researcher to gain an in-depth, holistic knowledge of the growth and development of the 15 feminist organizations under study. Qualitative methodology is seen as a form of exploratory-formulative research (Reid and Smith, 1981). It provides a richness of material which allows for data presentation in the form of quotation from subjects, examples of changes from actual documentation, and very little quantitative analysis (Reid and Smith, 1981).

Data Collection Method

The data collection method employed is known as the institutional method (Pennings, 1973). Data was obtained from two sources: from structured interviews and from documents made available to the researcher by the organizations. Archival documents are often used in organizational research (Pennings, 1973). Data obtained in this manner are labeled as objective (Pennings, 1973). Pennings (1973) states:

> obtaining information from documents reflecting the arrangement of positions such as the organizational chart, personnel department files, and job descriptions, or by interviewing some 'expert' such as the top manager, may be labeled 'objective. If the organizational charts of different organizations reveal different numbers of authority levels, then different degrees of centralization may be inferred (p. 687).

Structured interviews, a subjective form of measurement, with founders and executive directors provided an additional data source. By providing a second confirming data source, the researchers knowledge of the subject is enhanced. Price (1972) states:

> "Documents in surveys have different strengths and weaknesses and it is best to use both methods of data collection (plus observation) to comple-

ment each other rather to rely exclusively on a single method (p. 115).

In their study of the impact of organizational change on survival, Singh, House and Tucker (1986) used archival and interview-based data collection methods.

Data for this research study were collected from July 1989 to January 1990. The researcher made a site visit to each of the 15 organizations studied. Two to 6 hours were spent reading documents and interviewing personnel. A second site visit of from 1 to 3 additional hours to three of the organizations was required due to extensive documentation available to the researcher.

Documents examined by the researcher included published and unpublished articles, published books, articles of incorporation, bylaws, grant proposals, newspaper clippings, minutes of meetings of the board and staff, scrapbooks, newsletters, procedure and policy manuals, brochures, annual reports and interoffice memos.

As an additional data source, the researcher interviewed one or more original organization members and current leader from each organization. Figure 4 identifies each original organization member interviewed from each of the 15 organizations, as well as her original relationship and current relationship to the organization. Figure 5 identifies each current leader interviewed from each organization as well as his or her previous and current role in the organization.

To summarize Figure 4, at the organization's initial stage of development, nine out of those original organization members interviewed were founders of the organization, four volunteers and two were staff members. Of these 17 respondents, nine still currently connected to the organization. Six of the nine are either current executive directors or current board presidents of the organization. The other three are consultants or board members.

To summarize Figure 5, five of the current leaders had no previous role with the organization, while the other 10 current leaders were either founders, volunteers or staff members at a previous stage of the organization's development. Five of the current executive directors were original data collection method employed executive directors and founders.

For each variable, information obtained from an organization's archival and current documentation and interviews with original members and current leaders of the organization was recorded on an interview form (Appendix C) providing data for description and analysis of change over time. Data were collected from two points in the organization's life cycle, the initial stage of development (year one) and the current stage of development (current year). Data on each major study variable were collected in the following manner:

1. Goals

This variable is described by the types of goals (social change and client service) emphasized at an organization's initial and current stages of development. In order to describe this variable, data documenting the existence of and type of goals at two points in time, year one and in the current year of the organization's existence were recorded on a form (Appendix D). Interviews with original organization members and current leaders focused on these individuals' perceptions of goal emphasis at these two points in time.

2. Formalization

This variable is described by the existence of written rules, procedures, instructions, and communication documents at the organization's initial and current stages of development and their distribution to organization members.

In order to describe this variable, the existence of personal manuals, procedure manuals, job descriptions, organizational charts, minutes of staff meetings, and organization pamphlets and brochures were documented at two points in time, year one in the current year of the organization's existence. Interviews with original organization members and current leaders focused on their perceptions of the existence of these documents and the extent to which they were distributed to organization members at both points in time.

3. Personal Relationships

This variable is described by the importance of personal relationships at the organization's initial and current stage of development. In order to describe this variable, data were collected on the importance of personal relationships as documented in existing job descriptions at two points in time, year one and the current year of the organization's existence. Interviews with original organization members and current leaders focused on questions about the extent to which organization members knew each other through affiliations with the same feminist organizations previous to employment at this organization. Opinion of interviewees with respect to the extent of social contact outside of work as well as an encouragement to join other feminist organizations was obtained for the two points in time.

Name of Organization	Name of Founder or Historian	Initial Role	Current Role
BUCKS COUNTY			
A Woman's Place	Bev Frantz	Founder	Just left Board
Women for Sobriety	Jean Kirkpatrick	Founder and Exe. Director	Board Pres. and Exe. Dir.
CHESTER COUNTY			
Crime Victims' Center	Margaret Gusz	Founder	Exec. Director
Women's Suburban Clinic	Sherely Hollos	Founder	Exec. Director
DELAWARE COUNTY			
Domestic Abuse Project	Elaine Humme	Founder	None
Women Against Rape	Joyce Dale	Founder	Exec. Director
Women's Resource Center	Sue Staas	Original Volunteer	Board President
MONTGOMERY COUNTY The Birth Center	Sherely Hollos	Founder	Exec. Director
Women's Center of Montgomery County	Betty Sayre	Original Volunteer	Moved out of area
Victim Services Center	Kathy Riccio	Original Volunteer	Consultant
PHILADELPHIA COUNTY Interim House	Grace Walters	Original Staff Member	Consultant
Philadelphia Women's Network	Mary Brown	Founder	Board Member
Women in Transition	Lyn McMahon	Original Staff Member	None
Women Organized Against Rape	Jody Pinto Barbara Simon	Founder Orig. Volunteer	None
Women's Therapy Center	Sylvia Elias Patricia Mikols	Founder Founder	None None

Figure 3.3. Interviews with Original Organization Members

Name of Organization	Name of Current Leader	Previous Role	Current Role
BUCKS COUNTY			
A Woman's Place	Barbara Webber	None	Exec. Director
Women for Sobriety	Jean Kirkpatrick	Founder and Exe. Director	Board Pres. and Exe. Dir.
CHESTER COUNTY			
Crime Victims' Center	Margaret Gusz	Founder	Executive
Women's Suburban Clinic	Sherely Hollos	Founder	Exec. Director
DELAWARE COUNTY			
Domestic Abuse Project	Maxine Bailey	None	Exec. Director
Women Against Rape	Joyce Dale	Founder	Exec. Director
Women's Resource Center	Vivian Gutter	Original Volunteer	Volunteer
MONTGOMERY COUNTY			
The Birth Center	Elise Dormond	None	Director
Women's Center of Montgomery County	Donna Byrne	Volunteer	Exec. Director
Victim Services Center	Cynthia Gilhool	None	Exec. Director
PHILADELPHIA COUNTY			
Interim House	Robin Hornstein	None	Program Dir.
	William Hicks	Board Member	Board President
Philadelphia Women's Network	Nancy Pigford	Board Member	Board President
Women in Transition	Roberta Hacker	Staff Member	Exec. Director
Women Organized Against Rape	Karen Kulp	Staff Member	Exec. Director
Women's Therapy Center	Joan Biordi	Therapist	Administrator

Figure 3.4. Interviews with Current Leaders

4. Rewards

This variable is described by the type of rewards provided in the organization at the initial and current stages of development. In order to describe this variable, data were collected on the existence of material and non-material rewards as well as on the existence of differential pay for different job positions at two points in time, year one, and the current year of the organization's existence. Interviews with original organization members and current leaders focused on their perceptions of the rate of turnover for three different groups of organization members: volunteers; paid professional staff; and paid nonprofessionals staff; as well as longevity of key organization members. In addition, their perceptions of the level of the organization's salaries in comparison to other similar organizations in the community, was the obtained for these two points in time.

5. Divisions of Labor

This variable is described by the existence of discrete job positions at the organization's initial and current stages of development. In order to describe this variable, the number of discrete job titles were documented at two points in time, year one and the current year of the organization's existence. Interviews with original organization members and current leaders focused on their perceptions of how the work was divided, including any existing job rotation among organization members.

6. Authority Structures

This variable is described by the type of organizational structure identified at the organization's initial and current stages of development. In order to describe this variable, data were collected on the number of hierarchical levels existing at two points in time, year one, and the current year of the organization's existence. Interviews with original organization members and current leaders focused on questions about staff participation in the decision-making process in hiring and promoting staff as well as participation in decisions regarding adoption of new programs and new policies at these two points in time.

7. Environmental Factors

These variables (relationships with funding sources, interorganizational relationships, organizational growth and leadership changes) are described in association with the other six variables. In order to describe these variables, a form (Appendix E) documenting current information for these variables was used.

Conclusion

Information obtained from the data collected on each variable formed the individual case study for each feminist organization. Each case study examines in detail development of the organization and changes on the six dimensions (goals, formalization, personal relationships, rewards, division of labor and authority structure) over the organization's life cycle (Kimberly, 1980). Each case study describes the status of the major variables at the organization's inception, during his early life, during its evolution and in the organization as it is today. Special emphasis was placed on describing the organization at its initial stage of development during year one, and at its current stage of development. Chapter Four presents these case studies.

Chapter 4

Data Presentation

Introduction

This chapter presents case studies on each of the 15 feminist organizations studied. The framework for the case studies is an organizational life cycle model (Kimberly, 1980). By using a life cycle model, data on the evolution of each of the 15 feminist organizations studied is presented in a systematic format.

Each case study is organized to include the following periods in the organization's life cycle: a) the birth of the organization; b) the early life of the organization; c) the evolution of the organization; d) the organization as it is today; and, e) major highlights in the organization's life. For each period in the organization's life, the focus is on describing the variables presented in Chapter Three. The case studies are presented by county in alphabetical order. Figure 4.1 presents the case study presentation order.

A Woman's Place
The Birth of the Organization

In 1976, three women, who were part of a local Bucks County support group focusing on issues of domestic violence, opened a drop-in center for women. They invited a fourth woman to join their efforts, due to her grant-writing abilities. The center was originally located in a building owned by one of their spouses (B. Frantz, personal communication, November 20, 1989).

Their purpose in opening the center was to address the domestic violence issue by making the problem more visible to county officials. On Christmas Day, 1976, the police contacted one of the founders to refer an abused woman with two children, and subsequently, the center sheltered its first domestic violence client. From that point on, their focus changed from "making the center look pretty" to providing a safe place for abused women. Each founder committed up to one year of money and time to the center, A Woman's Place (B. Frantz, personal communication, November

BUCKS COUNTY
A Woman's Place
Women for Sobriety

CHESTER COUNTY
Crime Victims' Center of Chester County
Women's Suburban Clinic

DELAWARE COUNTY
Domestic Abuse Project
Women Against Rape
Women's Resource Center

MONTGOMERY COUNTY
The Birth Center
Women's Center of Montgomery County
Victim Services Center of Montgomery County

PHILADELPHIA COUNTY
Interim House
Philadelphia Women's Network
Women In Transition
Women Organized Against Rape
Women's Therapy Center

Figure 4.1. Case Study Presentation Order

The organization was incorporated in 1977 to:

establish, maintain, support and operate a multi-dimensional center or centers for women offering counseling, assistance, information, referral, workshops, seminars, conversation, education and support in general to all women; to develop a base of support and resources for abused women and women in general; to cooperate with federal, state and local government and agencies and with privately chartered organizations to insure the optimum use and application of all resources and services for abused women and women in general; to educate and inform the community and public about the abuse of women and their children, and about the needs and capabilities of women; the primary focus is to establish, maintain, support and operate a shelter(s), home(s), center(s), to provide emergency shelter, housing, and care, and treatment for abused women and their children for escape in time of domestic or marital violence or abuse and to provide for follow-up support, assistance, and counseling, that a woman may need to institute changes in her dangerous environment, and referrals to appropriate available professional and/or social agencies (A Woman's Place. <u>Articles of Incorporation</u>, February 7, 1977).

The Early Life of the Organization

The founders became the first Board of Directors. They and a handful of other volunteers ran the shelter. One of the founder's sisters became the volunteer director, due to her interest in the shelter as well as the proximity of her home to the shelter. The Board was consensual in their decision-making, taking turns as officers. They often spent many hours debating whether not they wanted to be part of the county social service system. In 1978, when the organization could not find another reliable funding source, the Board did agree to lease a building for the sheltering of domestic violence victims from the county for $1.00 per year. By securing a facility, the Shelter was able to ensure its survival. This action, however, resulted in a dependency on local funding which has continued since then (B. Frantz, personal communication, November 20, 1989).

In 1978, the volunteer director became the first paid director of the Shelter. It was necessary to do this to continue the Shelter's operation because of county service requirements. At this point, the organizational structure became hierarchical, with a few paid staff members taking on the direction of the volunteers. With the move to paid staff, differential pay existed among job positions (B. Frantz, personal communication, November 20, 1989).

After five years as director, the first director left to take a new position with the state's Domestic Violence Coalition. The position at the shelter was filled by one of the shelter staff members (B. Frantz, personal communication, November 20, 1989).

The Evolving Organization

The leadership style of the new director was considerably different from the former director's leadership style. The new director was authoritative and directive, while the former director delegated and distributed responsibility among organization members. At this point, the board, which had been a real working board, accepted the new director's style, as they were no longer able or willing to continue their active roles. In addition, within the board, a philosophical difference was deepening between board members interested in fund-raising and other external activities and those board members interested in the concrete issues of domestic violence. Many board members were interested in the day-to-day operation of the Shelter (B. Frantz, personal communication, November 20, 1989).

Programmatically, the Board and other members supported the Shelter model. The development of additional programs such as community education, support groups and court accompaniment were delegated as secondary to the maintenance of the Shelter. Serious problems, such as two rapes of women in the shelter and the resignation of the executive director, occurred during the 2-year time period between 1986 and 1988. (B. Frantz, personal communication, November 20, 1989).

This led to a large turnover in Board membership. In addition, the new director hired in 1988 remained with the organization for only three months. A new grievance procedure was instituted as a result of problems with her tenure and resignation. Until the summer of 1989, this leadership role was vacant. Three staff members who had been with the organization for more than five years led the organization in the day-to-day operation of the Shelter (B. Frantz, personal communication, November 20, 1989).

The Organization As It Is Today

In August 1989, after a national search for the position of director, a new director, former director of the Rape Crisis Center in California, was hired. She brought to A Woman's Place 20 years of experience in administering social change programs and organizations (A Woman's Place. A

Woman's Place Newsletter, Fall, 1989. Available from A Woman's Place, P.O. Box 299, Doylestown, PA, 18901). The Board consciously sought a leader from outside of the organization, in order to broaden the organization's perspective beyond shelter management. The Board required the qualification of a feminist orientation, with previous experience in feminist organization management for the director position (B. Frantz, personal communication, November 20, 1989).

Renovations of the Shelter were carried out, providing more separation of the staff from the residents. The county has given the organization an additional building across the street from the Shelter for administrative purposes. For the first time, administrative staff is physically separated from Shelter staff (B. Webber, personal communication, October 26, 1989).

Although the veteran staff have been supportive during the transition period, there is a feeling of alienation among new and old staff members, as well as among new and old Board members (B. Frantz, personal communication, November 20, 1989).

The organizational structure remains hierarchical, with nine full-time and five part-time staff members. There are 40 volunteers. The annual budget is $314,000. For the first time in the organization's history, there is operating deficit of $34,000. Board members are concentrating on raising more money so that the organization will not have to decrease the number of appointees and/or employee benefits (B. Webber, personal communication October 26, 1989). Currently, the major funding source for the organization is governmental (local, state and federal). United Way of Bucks County and the private sector in Bucks County provide some support for the organization (A Women's Place. Brochure, 1989).

Major Highlights in the Organization's Life

1976   Drop-in center started by four women

1977   Incorporation of A Women's Place

1978   First paid director (formerly volunteer director); move to county building for lease of $1.00/year

1982   Original paid director replaced by second paid director. Shift in management style from delegation to authoritative style

1986-88   Serious problems in Shelter culminating with director's res-
           ignation

1988   New director hired but resigned after only 3 months, griev-
           ance procedure put in place by Board

1989   National search for director; hiring of new director with pre-
           vious feminist management experience in August, 1989; board
           expectation of new director to expand perspective of organi-
           zation beyond Shelter

Women for Sobriety
The Birth of the Organization

Women for Sobriety was founded by Jean Kirkpatrick, Ph.D., herself
an alcoholic for 27 years. In 1973, she advocated a program exclusively
for a project for the female alcoholic to meet the differing needs of women.
Those needs, according to Dr. Kirkpatrick, are building up self-esteem
and self-worth while letting go of guilt. As a recovering person, she became dissatisfied with Alcoholics Anonymous, feeling that " women need
their own program - one without men" ("Organization Tackles Female
Problem Drinker," United Press International, 1976).

Using her own money, she placed classified ads in newspapers and
sent out a newsletter to advertise the program she originally called New
Life. The newsletter, Sobering Thoughts, a monthly publication, was to
be used in the New Life self-help group meetings. The New Life program
consisted of thirteen philosophical statements which, when accepted and
used in everyday life, have the power to change an individual's negative
outlook to a positive perspective on life. These thirteen Acceptance Statements have formed the core philosophy for the Women for Sobriety self-
help group program (Kirkpatrick, 1981.)

The Early Life of the Organization

In 1975, another woman, who was working with women's groups in
New York, helped Dr. Kirkpatrick market and establish the New Life
program. In July 1975, the program was incorporated as Women for Sobriety. The goal of Women for Sobriety is to help women overcome dependence upon alcohol through group therapy and monthly publications
(Kirkpatrick, 1981). Two support groups started simultaneously in

Westchester, New York, and Quakerstown, Pennsylvania. The organization intended to reach out to alcoholic women across the United States and internationally (J. Kirkpatrick, personal communication, July 31, 1989).

In 1976, a syndicated article in 55 newspapers across the nation helped to publicize the program. With a start-up grant of $43,000 from a local foundation, Dr. Kirkpatrick was able to respond to inquiries generated by the newspaper article by writing materials, the program booklet, the beginner's booklet, and an outline for the formation and leadership of the groups, for use in the groups (J. Kirkpatrick, personal communication, July 31, 1989).

The by-laws of the organization forbade the groups from reproducing the materials on their own and held the groups accountable to the national organization located in Quakerstown (Women for Sobriety. By-Laws, undated).

The purpose of the organization was stated as: to help women recover from problem drinking through the discovery of self, gained by sharing experiences, hopes, and encouragement with other women in similar circumstances. In addition, Women for Sobriety is unique in that it is an organization of alcoholic women for alcoholic women. It recognizes women's emerging role and their need for self-esteem and self-assurance to face today's challenges (Women for Sobriety. The Program Booklet, 1976).

The Evolving Organization

Dr. Kirkpatrick did not want the Board of Directors to gain control over the organization's development. The original Board of Directors was composed of influential women in Quakertown, whose husbands' names Dr. Kirkpatrick used to obtain her first grant. Although these women were her friends and they helped to write the initial materials for the Women for Sobriety groups, she decided not to rely on these relationships because there were too many strings attached. She dissolved her first Board of Directors and reformulated a national Board, composed of women who were Women for Sobriety group moderators and with herself as President. They meet yearly. All help in writing new material and updating existing materials for the groups (J. Kirkpatrick, personal communication, July 31, 1989).

Dr. Kirkpatrick decided not to seek any further foundation or public money but to depend solely on membership dues from the groups. She found that taking government money required the fulfillment of too many extraneous requirements. For example, the start-up money was restricted to Pennsylvania, whereas she envisioned the organization to be national in scope. In addition, the state wanted her to be a field representative under their auspices and she wanted to follow a self-help group model (J. Kirkpatrick, personal communication, July 31, 1989).

By 1979, Women for Sobriety had groups operating throughout the United States and in Canada. Group members' donations, her own speaking engagements, and income from the sale of her books enabled Women for Sobriety to purchase a printing press. Up until this time, Dr. Kirkpatrick operated the organization from her home. However, at this time, the organization's operations moved into a one-room storefront in Quakertown. This location became and remains the organization's headquarters (J. Kirkpatrick, personal communication, July 31, 1989).

Initially, Dr. Kirkpatrick and a part-time secretary were the only two organization staff members. In 1980, two additional part-time staff were hired to assist in the printing and distribution of the literature to all the Women for Sobriety groups. These additional staff became the group coordinator and the publisher. The part-time secretary became the administrative assistant (J. Kirkpatrick, personal communication, July 31, 1989). In 1980, Dr. Kirkpatrick decided, with her Board's approval, that each participant in each Women for Sobriety group would be charged a $2.00 attendance fee per group meeting. This, however, resulted in a decline in new groups and a decline in attendance at already existing groups. According to Dr. Kirkpatrick, 99 percent of the groups terminated when the $2.00 fee was instituted. It took 5 years to build the national organization back up to about 100 contributing groups registered with the main office. However, there is a continuing problem with the use of WFS literature by unregistered groups (J. Kirkpatrick, personal communication, July 31, 1989).

The Organization As It Is Today

The organization consisted of Dr. Kirkpatrick as the only full-time employee and three part-time employees. All are housed in the same room and there is frequent overlap of job responsibilities based on what must be done at the moment. Anyone will answer the telephone and assist with the newsletter. However, basic job assignments are held by each employee, although there are no written job descriptions (J. Kirkpatrick, personal communication, July 31, 1989).

There is a written organizational chart, with all paid positions reporting to the executive director. She makes the final decisions after discussing issues with staff members. As president of the board of directors, influence, and decision-making on the board level is ultimate as well (J. Kirkpatrick, personal communication, July 31, 1989).

The current budget is $110,000. Funding comes from membership fees (group and individual), speaking engagement fees and the sale of literature (there are now videotapes as well). As of January 1989, a new program targeted to overeaters has begun. According to Dr. Kirkpatrick, there are 10 groups participating in "New You" workshops, the overeaters program. The original Women for Sobriety literature continues to be used, but for the new groups, a change in the focus of the literature from alcohol abuse to overeating has been made (J. Kirkpatrick, personal communication, July 31, 1989).

The statement of purpose was reaffirmed in 1987. A Women for Sobriety motto was developed in 1988. The motto states: We are capable and competent, caring and compassionate, always willing to help another, bonded together and overcoming our addiction.

In an effort to control the group's development, regulated procedures for starting a group, as well as requirements for the leaders of the groups to be certified by Women for Sobriety and for the materials used to originate from Women for Sobriety are all recommended in a specific order and with specific intention by Women for Sobriety. In addition, treatment facilities are encouraged to use Women for Sobriety as a self-help portion of their treatment program (J. Kirkpatrick, personal communication, July 31, 1989).

Major Highlights in the Organization's Life

1973   Advertisement to determine the interest of a self-help program for women alcoholics

1975   Incorporation of Women for Sobriety with the help of other women who marketed Dr. Kirkpatrick's program

1976   Syndicated newspaper article bringing nationwide attention to WFS; first and only grant received; local Board of Directors dissolved; national Board of Directors formed

1980   Printing press purchased; moved into a storefront in

Quakertown where all publications are produced; fee instituted
for attendance at group meetings at each meeting

1980-85   Decline in start up of and attendance at groups

1987   Statement of purpose in 1976 reaffirmed

1988   Model For WFS developed; overeaters' groups started

The Crime Victim's Center of Chester County
The Birth of the Organization

In 1972, several Chester County women, who were members of the
National Organization for Women, participated together in a consciousness-raising (C-R) group focusing on the issue of sexual assault. As a
result of their interest in this issue, these women organized a county meeting to address the lack of services to sexual assault victims in the county.
In 1973, two of these women began the Rape Crisis Council of Chester
County, consisting of a hotline run out of a rented room at the local YWCA
(M. Gusz, personal communication, September 13, 1989). The goals of
the Rape Crisis Council were to provide supportive services to victims of
sexual assault/abuse (Rape Crisis Council. Charter, 1973).

The Early Life of the Organization

Initially, a steering Committee directed the Rape Crisis Council. Day-
to-day operations were run by these and other volunteers. Eventually, one
of the original founders became the executive director. Using the volunteer model of Women Organized Against Rape as their model for training
volunteers, the volunteers began providing the services of hospital counseling, prevention education, speaking engagements and court accompaniment, in addition to the hotline. The other founder then became a part-
time prevention education speaker for the organization (M. Gusz, personal communication, September 13, 1989).

The organization incorporated in 1977 as the Victim and Witness Assistance Services of Chester County. This change broadened and the
organization's goals to "provide a full range of supportive services to
victims of crime and their families . . . " (The Crime Victims' Center of
Chester County, Inc. Charter, July, 1977) rather than to just victims of
sexual assault. This decision occurred for two major reasons. First, there

had been a murder in Chester County and the Rape Crisis Center was asked by Chester County politicians to take the victim's family through the legal system. Secondly, new funding sources were becoming available for services to other types of victims (M. Gusz, personal communication, September 13, 1989).

The Evolving Organization

With increased funding, the organization moved to a larger facility. A Board of Directors was developed from the original Steering Committee. In 1986, the organization changed its name to Crime Victims' Center of Chester County, Inc. to reflect the comprehensive victims' service center it had become. Services to victims of sexual assault became one project of the organization (M. Gusz, personal communication, September 13, 1989).

Although the organization still receives Department of Public Welfare funding through the Pennsylvania Coalition Against Rape (PCAR), The Crime Victims' Center of Chester County, Inc. has issues with PCAR leadership According to Margaret Gusz, the organization's current executive director, the organization does not want to be identified as a feminist organization. In addition, the organization's leaders feel distribution of state funds is partial (M. Gusz, personal communication, September 13, 1989). Therefore, the organization withdrew their membership from the Pennsylvania Coalition against Rape (PCAR), although; the organization's founders were two of their original founders of PCAR.

The Organization As It Is Today

The current Executive Director (one of the two founders) took over from the other founder, who retired in April 1988. Previously, she had been the Project Director of the organization. There are currently eight paid staff, with one serving part-time. The organization is expanding the number of paid staff due to the expansion of the workload (M. Gusz, personal communication, September 13, 1989).

The emphasis has shifted to paid staff, with a decline in using volunteer staff to do professional work tasks. A minimum of a Bachelor's degree in social services or related field is now required for employment. Volunteers who originally did all jobs are used to supplement the provision of services by paid staff. The volunteer program is being revamped, due to the change in use of volunteers. The organization now has a greater need for volunteers at night. Those volunteers who enjoyed the social aspects of volunteering have dropped out. Current volunteer training reflects this shift in focus (M. Gusz, personal communication, September 13, 1989). Volunteers provide the following services: on-call to the sexual assault hotline; direct service to clients; prevention/education programs; professional/advisory training/in-service; meetings; and miscellaneous support (The Crime Victims' Center of Chester County, Inc. Annual Report, 1987-1988).

The authority has always been held by paid staff as the two founders moved from volunteer status to Executive Director and Project Director, the two highest level positions in the organization. Since moving to the Executive Director model, the organization has always been hierarchically structured, with decisions being made by management. One of the major problems is that salaries are not seen as competitive, particularly in the clerical area. This has contributed to a high turnover in the office manager position (M. Gusz, personal communication, September 13, 1989).

The budget is $273,000, with the largest amount of funding coming from a variety of government sources. There are no memberships. The organization is a constituent of five different United Ways (Avon Grove, Chester County, Kennett Area, Oxford Civic Association and Southeastern Pennsylvania) and does receive private foundation money (The Crime Victims' Center of Chester County, Inc. Annual Report, 1987-1988).

Major Highlights in the Organization's Life

1973   Rape Crisis Council of Chester County begins as hotline at local YM-YWCA

1976   LEAA funding terminated; need for additional funding sources

1977   Broadening of purpose to include victims of crimes other than sexual assault; incorporation with name change to reflect broader perspective

1986   Name change to Crime Victims' Center to reflect comprehensive nature of program

1988   Retirement of initial Executive Director (and original founder); Executive Directorship taken on by other founder

Women's Suburban Clinic
The Birth of the Organization

In 1973, the Supreme Court decision of Roe vs. Wade legalized abortion. Prior to the decision, in early 1973, Sherely Hollos spoke at the University of Pennsylvania about opening an abortion clinic. The women she spoke with suggested that she go to Planned Parenthood. It was through Planned Parenthood that she was introduced to Dr. Steven Ellen who agreed to become the medical director for the soon-to-be started abortion clinic that she envisioned (S. Hollos, personal communication, August 2, 1989).

Hollos took out a $8,000 loan, which the clinic was able to pay off later in 1973, and incorporate the Women's Suburban Clinic (WSC) located in Paoli, Chester County. The Articles of Incorporation (1973) state the purpose of the corporation as:

> to provide and promote medical care, and in particular, reproductive health care by the operation of a clinic on a non-profit basis and to the extent of its financial ability to provide services to those unable to pay fully, open to the members of the community, to perform under safe clinical conditions vasectomies and to terminate pregnancies in women up to the end of the first trimester and prior to the viability of the fetus by abortion performed under safe clinical conditions ... and also to educate and instruct by the dissemination of information and by counseling with regard to family planning, pregnancy control . . . (Women's Suburban Clinic, Articles of Incorporation, 1973).

Original Board minutes of 1973 reflect Hollos' intention to gain a reputation of being a small, personal, quiet clinic "where no one shall be turned away".

The Early Life of the Organization

Women's Suburban Clinic opened its doors on July 11, 1973 and immediately had patients. Services provided by the Clinic included first trimester abortions and free walk-in pregnancy testing. Due to the large numbers of patients receiving abortions, even at reduced payment rates, the Clinic was able to pay off its initial loan and has suffered very few monetary difficulties (S. Hollos, personal communication, August 2, 1989). Most referrals came from private physicians. Referrals from private physicians were encouraged by a direct mail campaign initiated by the Board of Directors who purchased mailing lists of doctors in Philadelphia, Chester, Delaware, and Montgomery counties. The original 11-person Board, all women, developed the brochure to send out. In addition, Planned Parenthood help with the publicity of the clinic by advertising it in their newsletter. CHOICE in Philadelphia also lent it supports to Women's Suburban Clinic and referred women to the Clinic.

The majority of Women's Suburban Clinic patients have always been private pay rather than medical assistance patients, due to the referral sources as well as to the limitations of medical assistance subsidize abortions since 1977. Vasectomies were going to be offered, but due to a disagreement with the doctor who was to perform them, the service was never initiated. Many-laparotomies are offered. (S. Hollos, personal communication, August 2, 1989).

In addition to Sherely Hollos, who served as the part-time executive director and Dr. Ellen, the original staff included several other part-time employees: nurses (LPNs and RNs), medical assistance, and counselors. There were some volunteers from Planned Parenthood and the Junior League who helped in the counseling and reception areas. However, due to the stressful nature of the interaction between patient and volunteer, the use of volunteers was discontinued at an early stage. Volunteers were replaced by paid staff (S. Hollos, personal communication, August 2, 1989).

In 1975, a nurse clinician was added to the staff. She suggested that services be expanded to include gynecological services and family planning. The Board approve the suggestion for implementation on a limited basis the following year. It was decided that, if patients ask about gynecological or follow-up services, they could receive them at the Clinic (Women's Suburban Clinic. Minutes of Board Meeting, June 6, 1977). WSC was and remains a very specialized organization with clear job responsibilities based on profession: nurses (several categories) and, added in 1975, MSW and BSW social workers as counselors (S. Hollos, personal communication, August 2, 1989).

The Evolving Organization

The expanding programs of Women's Suburban Clinic required more staff and created a space problem for the Clinic. Due to tension between Women's Suburban Clinic and the other tenants who felt that WSC hindered their own operation at that location, Women's Suburban Clinic could not obtain a lease. In 1978, however, the organization did receive a five-year lease and took over the entire first floor of the building where they have remained. This lease was renewed again in 1983 (S. Hollos, personal communication, August 2, 1989).

In 1980, the political activities of the Right-to-Life movement took the form of protest outside of the office building. This escalated to a climax in 1984, when Women's Suburban Clinic offices were broken into by the protesters. Women's Suburban Clinic filed a court suit, which resulted in limitation of the number of protesters to three outside the building at any given time. The continued presence of picketers outside of the building is very stressful to staff as well as to patients. To enhance the morale of the staff and to train them to deal with the protesters, Women's Suburban Clinic provides frequent in-service training and constant mutual support (S. Hollos, personal communication, August 2, 1989).

In addition to the private group protest against abortion, federal government regulations on payment for abortions has become increasingly tight. By 1985, government subsidized payments for abortions were almost non-existent. Although the cost of an abortion increased, the Clinic intended to offer reduced rates and loans to those who could not afford to pay. The majority of those seeking abortions were private pay patients not covered by medical insurance. The Board was motivated to expand its membership to include more individuals from the West Chester-Paoli Area, which they felt would help to provide a stable position for the Clinic in the community. However, there was more turnover in staff and board members, due to the political atmosphere and pressure to become more politically active in advocating for reproductive rights. Since 1984, Women's Suburban Clinic has changed its fund-raising appeal from emphasis on education to emphasis on support for its Legal Defense Fund. (S. Hollos, personal communication, August 2, 1989).

The Organization As It Is Today

The organization is divided into several departments. The counseling department has evolved into a major component in addition to the medical department. In addition to the medical director, there is a clinic administrator. The organization is hierarchically designed. There are 26 employees (18 of whom work part-time). Decisions are made at the administrative level and above. Individuals and all levels are involved in some aspect of the decision-making process through participation in the bi-weekly staff meetings (S. Hollos, personal communication, August 2, 1989).

Since 1987, Women's Suburban Clinic has become extremely specialized in its counseling services. Therapists must have a graduate degree, post-graduate training and active membership in a professional association, the Center for Contextual Therapy and Allied Studies. Therapy at Women's Suburban Clinic is geared to building trust and fairness in relationships. Therapy is geared towards helping patients cope with issues like stress, decision making, grief/loss, addictive behaviors, depression and wounded or disappointing relationships (Women's Suburban Clinic, Counseling Services, undated).

Women's Suburban Clinic is on the verge of offering anonymous AIDS testing to both men and women. As of September 1989, the organization's first proposal for government funding in the area of AIDS testing is being prepared (S. Hollos, personal communication, August 2, 1989).

The philosophy statement was rewritten in 1987 to state:

> Women's Suburban Clinic is a feminist, private non-profit clinic that provides all women who seek its services with all relevant and psychological choices for themselves. As a feminist clinic, Women's Suburban Clinic is committed to treating the staff with the same respect it gives its clients, to participatory management, to equitable compensation for the staff and to providing the staff with the opportunity for growth and self knowledge. The philosophy guides the pregnancy testing, all phases of counseling, options counseling ... and educational services (Women's Suburban Clinic. Philosophy Statement, 1987).

The current budget of Women's Suburban Clinic is $800,000. Funding consists of fee-for-service, with a small United Way donor option allocation of under $5,000 in the minimal funds received from fundraising mail appeals. The abortion fee is now $245.00. The original fee in 1973 was $155.00, which was reduced after the first year and then increase to reach its current level (S. Hollos, personal communication, August 2, 1989).

The majority of the staff are part-time (Women's Suburban Clinic. Minutes of Board Meeting, January 23, 1989). The executive director and the medical director positions have always been part-time (S. Hollos, personal communication, August 2, 1989). The focus of the staff has become much more advocacy-related, because of the political atmosphere in Pennsylvania. Women's Suburban Clinic often sponsors buses to Harrisburg and Washington, D.C. for Pro-Choice rallies. Sherely Hollos is the leader of that activism among the staff and encourages them to do more for reproductive rights (S. Hollos, personal communication, August 2, 1989). Women's Suburban Clinic has begun a newsletter to disseminate information on the status of abortion rights and the ways in which others can support the legality of abortions (Women's Suburban Clinic. Newsletter, July 1989. Available from Women's Suburban Clinic, East Paoli Medical Park, 1440 Russell Road, Paoli, PA 19301).

Major Highlights In the Organization's Life

1973   Supreme Court decision legalizing abortions; WSC opens

1976   First Joint Conference on abortions sponsored by the four area abortion clinics

1977   Services increased to include gynecological and family planning

1978   New 5-year lease for expanded room in building; alleviation of poor staff morale due to cramped space

1980-84   Increased protests by private citizens against abortions and for right to life; culmination in law suite and limiting of picketing to three at any given time

1985-89   Decreased government support for the legality of abortions; increased protests led by executive director by supporters of pro-choice; expansion of program-contextual therapy counseling program and AIDS/HIV anonymous testing

Domestic Abuse Project
The Birth Of the Organization

In 1971, a group of women gathered to form the Women's Action Coalition (WAC) of Delaware County. Initially, the women came together to celebrate the 52nd anniversary of the passage of the Amendment to the Constitution, the suffrage amendment. They continued to meet to form consciousness-raising groups, which evolved into action committees. In 1975, two of these women formed the Women in Transition committee, which initially emphasized marital crisis, but quickly shifted to marital abuse, reflecting the needs of other women in the community (Benson, 1980).

The founder of the Marital Abuse Project (MAP) was herself going through a divorce and found her own involvement with the Women's Action Coalition to be empowering. She wanted to make the positive experience known to other women. However, after the brutal death of a woman as a result of a beating from her husband, the victim's lawyer asked this chapter of the Marital Abuse Project committee to address the problem of battered wives in Delaware County (E. Humme, personal communication, September 12, 1989).

The Marital Abuse Project (MAP) was a project of the Women's Action Coalition and was housed in the same location as the Senior Citizens' Safety project in the Women Against Rape Project of Women's Action Coalition (Benson, 1980).

The Early Life of the Organization

A grant was written and accepted by the Pennsylvania Governor's Justice Commission for funding the Marital Abuse Project separate from the other two Women's Action Coalition projects, Women Against Rape and the Senior Citizens' Safety project. The goals of the organization were stated as:

> immediate and continuous support to victims of marital abuse; liaison with police, courts, the district attorney's office and hospitals to gain understanding and cooperation in dealing with marital abuse; to study the occurrence and existing institutional response to marital abuse in Delaware County, in order to find more effective methods of intervention; to work toward changes in the legal system which will protect victims from abusive spouses; and to educate the community and social agencies to the needs and problems of abused spouses (Marital Abuse Project. Grant proposal to the Pennsylvania Governor's Justice Commission, 1976).

The program was initiated with staffing by the two co-founders, who volunteered until this first grant of $20,000 was received from the Justice Commission. These individuals' then became part-time paid staff members and enlisted the help of 10 volunteers. The jobs were divided among all and the organization was formed as a collective. One of the founder's recalled that they met together each week to make decisions and distribute the work according to skill, interests, resources and time. Each time a problem became apparent, they sat down and worked out an appropriate policy (E. Humme, personal communication, September 12, 1989).

The Marital Abuse Project incorporated in December 1977. The first program was a hotline. In 1976, they answered 748 hotline calls. The founders decided not to open the Shelter due to the passing of legislation which protected battered women in their own homes. Instead, where needed, the organization provided temporary emergency housing and volunteer private homes, known as safe homes, to women who were unable to remain in their own homes. Support groups and educational services were provided as well. The two co-founders of the Marital Abuse Project were a major influence in the organizing of the statewide coalition, Pennsylvania Coalition Against Domestic Violence, organized in 1976 and the National Coalition Against Domestic Violence, established in 1978 (E. Humme, personal communication, September 12, 1989).

The Evolving Organization

In the spring of 1977, a District Justice requested that the Marital Abuse Project Place a volunteer at the courthouse in order to accompany and council women who were victims of violence in their homes. In May 1978, one volunteer was placed in a satellite office at the courthouse in the city of Chester. Due to demand, her volunteer hours were immediately increased from one morning per week to five mornings per week (E. Humme, personal communication, September 12, 1989).

In 1980, the organization changed its name to Domestic Abuse Project (DAP) in order to extend services to any adults living in a violent family situation, not just victims of marital abuse. The specific purposes of the corporation were then restated as:

> to provide services to victims of domestic violence, services shall include crisis telephone counselors and/or temporary shelter for the victim and her dependent children and/or professional counseling . . . to conduct educational and other efforts to inform residents of Delaware County about the extent and character of domestic violence and to inform victims of domestic violence of their legal rights and remedies. . . ; to conduct educational and other efforts to inform legislators, police, courts, social service organizations and mental health agencies of the multiple needs of victims of domestic violence and to work with these organizations to develop and expand resources and services for victims of domestic violence; and to engage in any and all lawful act which will . . . contribute to the elimination of domestic violence (E. Humme. Title XX Proposal, 1980).

In 1980, one of the co-founders holding the position of co-director left the organization. The board of directors declined to continue the co-directorship model, although the remaining co-founder advocated for it.

The board had also been expanded to include male community members who were influencing the direction of the agency in a more traditional way, such as to dissolving the co-directorship model. (The initial makeup of the board had consisted of four like-minded community members and three staff members.) Decision-making continued to be accomplished collectively; everyone had to concur in order for the group to move on from discussion of one issue to the next. They could disagree, but not to the point that the organization was not able to move forward (E. Humme, personal communication, September 12, 1989).

Subsequently in 1980, the Board was restructured, with the Executive Director and other staff no longer serving as board members. The collective decision-making process was terminated, leaving the more traditional separation between board and staff. The collective structure was replaced with a hierarchical structure. In 1983, a management team was formed, consisting of the Executive Director, the Fiscal Coordinator, the Program Coordinator and the three Site Coordinators (E. Humme, Title XX Proposal, 1983).

From inception, volunteers played a major role in the service provision of the organization. They did everything paid staff did and were always given priority in hiring. However, as the organization expanded programmatically with the opening of the shelter in 1984 and the annual budget and number of paid staff increased, the status of the volunteers declined. Issues of volunteers feeling devalued, questions about the value of their work and their importance in the decision-making process, and difficulty in replacing volunteers who become paid staff were common in recurring themes. One way the Domestic Abuse Project confronted these issues was by holding retreats and providing in-service training. In addition, in 1987, the volunteers established a Volunteer Empowerment Council. This Council acts as the voice of the volunteers to other members of the organization. Volunteers are also members of the Board Committees, which are also composed of Board Members, and paid staff members (E. Humme, personal communication, September 12, 1989).

The organization has struggled with its decision-making structure since its inception as a collective. In 1983, a management team approach to decision-making was instituted. Along with the management team, the program team and a legal team were developed with a coordinator of each team. The coordinator was responsible for direct service as well as leading the decision-making process of the team. However, this was not considered an effective structure, as paid staff complained that they were overworked, had too great a caseload and not enough time to complete their work, while volunteers continued to feel a lack of power. There were resignations on the part of paid staff. The organization struggled to find a structure that would accommodate the empowerment model on which the agency was founded (E. Humme, personal communication, September 12, 1989).

Funding sources increased. The Domestic Abuse Project became part of Women's Way in 1980. Program expansion took place, with new programs for children in the shelter. The executive director resigned in 1987. A co-director model was tried for a short period of time until a national search brought in the current executive director in October 1987 (E. Humme, personal communication, September 12, 1989).

The Organization As It Is Today

The current executive director continues to struggle with the organization's structure. She, along with the board committee formed to explore this issue, decided that adding a layer to the hierarchy would help to alleviate the major complaints with respect to work overload. There are currently four hierarchical levels: executive director, director, coordinator and counselor. Volunteers and students report to the coordinators or the director of the team to which they are assigned (Domestic Abuse Project. Organizational Chart, 1989).

Decision-making primarily involves the Board and Executive Director and/or members of the management team. Policy decisions are Board decisions. Program decisions are made by the management team, although input from the rest of the members of the organization is sought by the Board and Executive Director (M. Bailey, personal communication, August 23, 1989).

The current budget of the Domestic Abuse Project is $574,543. Government funding is the largest single fiscal source. There are 27 paid employees and 100 volunteers. Currently, volunteer training, which follows volunteer recruitment, is held four times a year. Of the 27 paid staff, 18 work full time and nine work part-time. Although there are men on the board of directors, there are no male employees (E. Humme, personal communication, September 12, 1989).

The newest position of Community Education and Training Director reflects the emergent emphasis on prevention activities. Previously, this role has been shared by all staff which frequently resulted in diversion of energy from direct service and confusion with respect to the role of volunteer coordinator (M. Bailey, personal communication, August 23, 1989). In addition, the organization is decentralizing to a second location, Upper

Darby, using funds from a new grant it has received. Domestic Abuse Project will be working with the Upper Darby township to develop a program for victims of domestic violence and that specified target area. The organization is currently in a growth period. (M. Bailey, personal communication, August 23, 1989).

Major Highlights In the Organization's Life

1971   Women's Action Coalition formed

1975   Women in Transition committee formed as part of the WAC

1976   Marital Abuse Project incorporated as separate entity

1977   Satellite opened in Chester court house

1980   Name change to Domestic Abuse Project; co-director leaves, organization becomes an affiliate of Women's Way

1984   Shelter opened

1987   Resignation of one original director; organization run by co-directors temporarily until a new director hired

1989   A new site in Upper Darby, in addition to the current Media location, with the new project targeted to that area, is funded

Delaware County Women Against Rape (WAR)
The Birth of the Organization

In 1971, the Women's Action Coalition (WAC) of Delaware County had become an interest of two women who subsequently were the co-founders of Women against Rape (WAR). Initially, these women participated in local consciousness-raising groups, but soon became active in action projects using a committee structure (J. Dale, personal communication, January 4, 1990).

The legal committee, of which these Women Against Rape founders were members, addressed issues of sex discrimination, employment discrimination and rape. In 1974, this committee began to explore Philadelphia's program, Women Organized Against Rape (WOAR) as a model for their own rape crisis program. It was suggested by the women at WOAR that the women from Delaware County meet with the Delaware County Assistant District Attorney, who had been supportive of Philadelphia's program (J. Dale, personal communication, January 4, 1990).

Their initial idea for a program focused on court accompaniment of rape victims; however, the district attorney pushed for the development of a comprehensive program offering hospital linkage and crisis counseling, as well as court accompaniment. A scant two months after this meeting, a grant proposal to the Law Enforcement Assistance Administration (LEAA) was written and submitted by the legal committee of the Women's Action Coalition. In 1974, the proposal was accepted by the Law Enforcement Assistance Administration; Women Against Rape became one of the projects of the Women's Action Coalition. The two co-founders became the co-directors (J. Dale, personal communication, January 4, 1990).

The Early Life of the Organization

The steering committee of Women's Action Coalition decided that the WAR project could address the additional women's issues of senior safety and marital abuse by obtaining additional government monies. The two projects, Senior Safety Project and the Marital Abuse Project, were eventually funded and became additional Women's Action Coalition projects. All three projects were housed in the same building. By 1976, each Women's Action Coalition project grew too large to remain simply parts of Women's Action Coalition. It was feared that funding potential was diluted by the three projects relying on one funding source (J. Dale, personal communication, January 4, 1990).

Also in 1976, Delaware County Women Against Rape (WAR) incorporated as a separate organization and composed its own organizational goals and objectives:

A. To increase reporting, prosecution, and conviction for rape and other sexual assaults;

B. To provide quality, comprehensive direct services to victims of rape and sexual assault, including: 1. Advocating for prompt and complete medical care for the victim in an emotionally supportive atmosphere; 2. Providing medical accompaniment to victims; 3. Providing assistance and support during police interviews and accompaniment to all legal proceedings; 4. Providing supportive, problem solving counseling to victims of rape and sexual assault; 5. Providing counseling to significant others.

C. To provide technical assistance and training to professionals and related disciplines such as police, medical personnel, and prosecutors;

D. To work toward changes in the legal system, particularly Pennsylvania rape law, which would provide compensation to the rape victim including, but not limited to, legal, medical, financial, and psychological restitution . . . (Women Against Rape. Organizational Goals and Objectives, undated).

Also in 1976, a Board of Directors was formed. One of the co-directors became president of the Board. The other co-director became Executive Director of the organization. These two women have remained in their respective positions since 1976. The move to one director was a result of accommodation to the demands of government funding (J. Dale, personal communication, January 4, 1990).

The Evolving Organization

The organization was approached by government funding sources as well as members of the Delaware County political system to serve victims of other crimes. However the Board, along with the Executive Director, made the decision not to succumb to these outside pressures and have kept their focus specific to victims of sexual assault. When LEAA funding ended, the organization was able to obtain funding from private foundations as well as different government sources. The establishment of the statewide coalition, Pennsylvania Coalition Against Rape, in 1976, facilitated successful negotiation for state monies to be distributed to each of the individual rape crisis organizations. The security provided by consistent funding source assisted WAR in resisting a transformation into a comprehensive victims' center (J. Dale, personal communication, January 4, 1990).

The Organization As It Is Today

The current organizational budget is $256,000. There are eight full-time employees, which include the Executive Director, a Program Director, five counselors and secretary. The secretary became a full-time employee in 1989. WAR has always operated as a hierarchical organization with decision-making power in the hands of the executive director and board of directors (J. Dale, personal communication, January 4, 1990). WAR has always utilized volunteers. However, these volunteers supplement the work of the paid staff. The philosophy of the founders was and remains that the clients are better served by professional staff. Volunteers fill in when paid staff are unavailable during the work day, and at night and on weekends. A quarterly newsletter has been developed for the volunteers in an effort to help them feel more closely affiliated to the organization. In addition, for the first time, a membership campaign is taking place. WAR's Board is also doing more long-range planning. Salary increments are being considered based on education and experience. Currently, equal increments are given to all paid staff. Also under consideration is a move into a larger building which would house all the victims' programs in Delaware County (J. Dale, personal communication, January 4, 1990).

Major Highlights in the Organization's Life

1971   Founders became involved in Women's Action Coalition; became leaders in legal committee

1974   Women Against Rape became Project of Women's Action Coalition

1976   Women Against Rape incorporated as separate organization; co-director model change to one executive director one president of board

1976-89   Original founders remain in same positions; board involved in long range planning issues

Women's Resource Center
The Birth of the Organization

In the spring of 1974, three members of a women's support group at a church in Wayne, Pennsylvania placed an ad in two local newspapers announcing an open meeting to discuss the possibility of developing a women's center. Forty-five women attended the meeting, one of whom is the current board president. She was so impressed with the ideas and energy of the group that she along with 11 other women, formed a planning committee to begin the process of establishing a women's center in Wayne (S. Stass, personal communication, December 4, 1989).

Out of this initial meeting the following need surfaced: 1) a physical space in which to meet and plan together; 2) a systematized body for gathering information and making referrals; and, 3) workshops in support groups to address important issues (N. Hopkins. Early WRC History, undated. Available from Women's Resource Center, P.O. Box 309, Wayne, PA 19087).

The church the women were affiliated with approved their request to use the room in the church building and a startup grant from the American Association of University Women (AAUW) allowed the Women's Resource center to open its doors in 1975. At that time, the first referral directories consisted of one blue notebook (N. Hopkins. Early WRC History, undated. Available from Women's Resource Center, P.O. Box 309, Wayne, PA 19087).

The mission statement of the organization was:

> [WRC is] dedicated to providing a structure which enables women to gain mutual support and strength to shape their own futures and become active in restructuring society. The goal is to help women achieve their full potential by providing a supportive environment, an educational forum and access to community resources (Women's Resource Center, Brochure, 1975).

The first services were referrals, educational information, and discussion groups (in the format of consciousness-raising groups). The Women's Resource Center was opened one day a week in the beginning (Women's Resource Center, Brochure, 1975).

The Early Life of the Organization

In its early years, the organization was run as a volunteer collective with no paid staff and no board of directors. Five women comprise the original collective. The decisions were made by them as a group; they all had to agree on a decision. An advisory board was dissolved soon after its formation because it was ineffective in carrying out its role (S. Stass, personal communication, December 4, 1989).

A positive response from area women increase the number of service days to three. Members of the collective worked hard to spread the word about the Center. Flyers were mailed throughout the area and the showing of films on Women's issues at the Center was advertised in local shopping centers, at the church and in local newspapers. The founders became very attuned to the needs of the women who came to the Center. After a film, they would hold small group discussions and ask the attendees for general programming ideas. The number of telephone calls for information and referral was increasing so that the collective members recognized the need for additional volunteers to increase the number of service days at the Center (N. Hopkins. Early WRC History, undated. Available from Women's Resource Center, P.O. Box 309, Wayne, PA19087).

The Evolving Organization

In 1977, the organization incorporated in order to accommodate funding requirements of the United Way from which it sought a grant. Also at this time, the original collective disbanded - one woman went to graduate school, another became the director of a woman's shelter and the third moved from the area. However, one of the initial founders and another woman from the church, where the Center is located, became volunteer co-directors and kept the organization going. At the time of incorporation, a board of directors was formed (S. Stass, personal communication, December 4, 1989).

One of the co-directors left after three year and another woman filled her position. During this time, the organization experienced a growth spurt

the office became systematic, we developed memberships, volunteer training took place regularly; we won United Way Community Development monies; and put together the first Woman Works art show..." (N. Hopkins. Early WRC History, undated. Available from Women's Resource Center, P.O. Box 309, Wayne, PA 19087).

After three years, both volunteer co-directors had left. The organization hired its first paid staff member as a full-time director (S. Stass, personal communication, December 4, 1989).

Growth continued, with the budget of the organization increasing from $24,000 to $60,000 over the next three years (1982-1985). The organization's paid staff grew in number as well. A paid part-time volunteer coordinator develop a secure core of 25 volunteers. Programmatically, therapists and lawyer referral list were developed (S. Stass, personal communication, December 4, 1989).

When the United Way grant ended in 1985, the organization was not able to obtain substitute funding and the director's position became a part-time. At this time, the director left the organization and the organization was without a director for nine months. A replacement hired in 1986 remain for only 9 months and was again replaced by another. Both of these replacements were affiliated with the church in which the organization is located. This replacement remained for 2 years, but had leadership and financial difficulties in her role as director (S. Stass, personal communication, December 4, 1989).

The Organization As It Is Today

The organization is currently in dire financial difficulties and continues to have difficulties at the director level. In the last year, two new programs, House-Sharing and Single Mothers Resources and Support Group, were funded but WRC is currently experiencing problems obtaining repeat funding for these programs. The Board has also had trouble in its fund-raising efforts. The current budget is $32,500. The board president has stated that, in order to survive, the organization needs $50,000 for the current fiscal year (Women's Resource center. Newsletter, September/October, 1989. Available from Women's Resource Center, P.O. box 309, Wayne, PA 19087).

In the fall of 1989, both the director and the volunteer coordinator resigned. The organization currently has no director. The one remaining part-time paid staff, the referral coordinator, and volunteer are in charge. Although the paid staff member has assumed the title of Acting Director, in reality, it is the volunteer, who is also a board member, who has greater control over the day-to-day operations (S. Stass, personal communication, December 4, 1989).

The current struggle for power and control between paid and volunteer staff began with previous director's movement away from the volunteer model. That director desired to hire more staff and give this staff more authority over volunteers. However, the volunteers felt that the director was not sensitive to volunteer needs, work habits or desires. The Board supported the volunteers feelings. The director ultimately resigned (S. Stass, personal communication, December 4, 1989).

The Board continues to struggle with this issue of power and ownership of the organization. They're looking at ways to alleviate the tensions between paid staff and volunteers. One solution under consideration is a volunteer contract which clearly identifies the responsibilities and accountability of volunteers, enabling paid staff to assume more control of the decision-making of the organization. A search for a new part-time director is underway. The continuing major concern of the organization is lack of funding. The primary service of the organization, information and referral, for which they receive over 3000 calls per year, has no consistent and apparent funding stream. Without funding, organization cannot continue (S. Stass, personal communication, December 4, 1989).

Major Highlights In the Organization's Life

1974   Organization begun by three women from a local church

1975   Services initiated one day per week in room in church

1977   Incorporated; Began seeking UW funds; volunteer coach directors take up leadership roles

1982   First paid director; establishment of UW funding; Growth spurt began

1985   UW funding terminated; Resignation of director; 9 months without director

1986   New part-time director hired; Tenure of new director lasted only nine months; No substitution for United Way funding obtained

1986-88 Agency struggling with no stable funding; To new programs initiated; but funding the programs not obtain

1989   Director and volunteer coordinator leave; Funding problems continue

The Birth Center
The Birth Of the Organization

The Birth Center (TBC) was founded by the founder of Women's Suburban Clinic (WSC). In 1977, she began paving the way for a birthing center separate from the abortion clinic as the Board of Women's Suburban Center did not want a birth center ancillary to the abortion clinic. In 1978, the Birth Center was incorporated as a free standing birthing center, the first in the Delaware Valley, with the Board of Directors different from that of the Women's Suburban Clinic. The initial Board of Directors coalesced as a result of their interest in the idea of the birth center (S.

Hollos, personal communication, August 2, 1989).

The incorporation occurred in August, 1978 with the following purposes:

> To operate a birth center where women will be delivered of children under the immediate direction of certified nurse-midwives and under the general direction of certified gynecologist/obstetricians and pediatricians; to qualify as a hospital and to provide prenatal, delivery and post-partum care to women; the facility is open to the community to provide a home setting for safe satisfying care to families anticipating a normal childbirth (The Birth Center. Articles of Incorporation, August 28, 1978).

The Board of Directors of WSC did approve granting. The Birth Center had an initial start-up grant of $48,000 and continued to support TBC financially until 1988 (S. Hollos, personal communication, August 2, 1989).

The Early Life of the Organization

The Birth Center opened in October 1979 in Bryn Mawr, Montgomery County. It is located in a Victorian style, three story red-brick house right around the corner from Bryn Mawr hospital. The home-like building was rented to the organization by one of its board members, who was also its first director of midwifery. Nine of the 12 original Board members were women (The Birth Center. Articles of Incorporation, August 28th, 1978). In addition to the director of midwifery, a full-time position, the Executive Director of Women's Suburban Clinic served as the Executive Director and the Women's Suburban Clinic Medical Director was the medical Director at The Birth Center on a part-time basis. They were both working part-time as well at the Women's Suburban Clinic. The original staff was also composed of a part-time administrator and a part-time Director of Newborn Care, a housekeeper and a part-time delivery assistant. The first baby was delivered in February, 1980 (E. Dormond, personal communication, July 26, 1989).

Financially, in addition to Women's Suburban Clinic, the organization depended entirely on payments (third-party payments accepted) by patients. It took 3 years to obtain the approval of one grant proposal by a private foundation for The Birth Center's general support. However, private foundation grants did not prove to be a consistent source or a large source of income for the Center. The organization's financial stability has always been fragile (S. Hollos, personal communication, August 2, 1989). In January 1981, the organization expanded its initial purpose to include "well-women health care", including complete gynecological care and family planning. Hiring of more part-time staff, in particular nursing, follow this expansion (The Birth Center. Minutes of Board Meeting, January, 1981).

The Evolving Organization

In 1982, the original director of Midwifery left the organization. The authority structure with a decision-making equal power of all directors created a conflict between the Director of Midwifery and the Medical Director. When decisions were to be made, the medical director usually won out. The lines of communication between these two positions opened up once this individual left. In order to increase public awareness of the Center, a newsletter was started in 1982 (S. Hollos, personal communication, August 2, 1989).

The organization also grew into a more hierarchical structure due to increased volume of births; more educational programs including postnatal programs; more staff positions and more staff at each position. Staff positions, such as Head nurse and registered nurse have been added, although mainly on a part-time basis. These positions are accountable to the Director of Midwifery (The Birth Center. Organizational Chart of the Birth Center, April 18, 1988).

Due to the specialized nature of the work of the organization, jobs are also very specialized and have specific educational and experiential requirements. Volunteers are women who have formally given birth at The Birth Center. They do fund-raising, publicity, staff at the front desk at night, and help with clerical task (E. Dormond, personal communication, July 26, 1989).

In 1983, the organization opened an office in Chester County to reach out to women and their families who could be seen for routine health care appointments' closer to home. The board decided to remain at the original location and purchase the home from its owners in 1985 (E. Dormond, personal communication, July 26, 1989).

The Organization As It Is Today

In 1988, the original founder and director decided to reduce her involvement at the Birth Center as executive director so that she could become more politically active in the area of reproductive rights at Women's Suburban Clinic (S. Hollos, personal communication, August 2, 1989). A new full-time position of director was added. This position, responsible to the Executive Director, oversees the day-to-day administrative functions of the Birth Center as well as board development, fund-raising and public relations. The position requires qualifications of a Bachelor's degree with minimal 5 years experience in a supervisory capacity with a volunteer health agency or in management of the small company. Understanding of and support for midwifery and the philosophy of the Birth Center is also desired (The Birth Center, Director Job Description, 1988). The first director was hired in 1988 (E. Dormond, personal communication, July 26, 1989).

For the first time in its existence, The Birth Center is supporting itself without financial help from Women's Suburban Clinic. Although the primary source of revenue is from fees for service, the organization now receives United Way donor option funds and limited private foundation grants and has its own fund-raisers. It is continuing to expand its educational programs to parents and to the community. The Birth Center is in the process of negotiating for a grant for a teenage pregnancy program from a private foundation (E. Dormond, personal communication, July 26, 1989).

The budget is now almost $500,000. There are approximately 160 births per year. There are seven full-time staff and 15 part-time staff, with key positions of Director, Director of Midwifery, receptionists and business manager full-time. One of the current board concerns is building expansion which is in the beginning stages. The other primary issue of concern to the administration is the negotiation of staff privileges for the midwives at Bryn Mawr Hospital (E. Dormond, personal communication, July 26, 1989).

Major Highlights In the Organization's Life

1978   The Birth Center Incorporated

1979   Services initiated with grant from WSC

1980   First baby born; first foundation money

1982   Resignation of original Director of Midwifery; organizational structure changed to hierarchy; Incorporated well woman health care and into program; Newsletter began

1985   Bought the birth center building

1988   Reduction of role of Executive Director and hiring a full-time Director; Financial independence from WSC for first-time

1989   10th anniversary; building expansion; Negotiation underway for privileges for midwives on staff at Bryn Mawr Hospital

Women's Center of Montgomery County
The Birth of the Organization

In September 1975, a general meeting of Montgomery County community women was held in the Abington library. The meeting was called as a result of a needs assessment telephone survey by the American Association of University Women (AAUW) regarding women's educational and job needs and the need for a Women's Center in Montgomery County area. Over 100 women attended. Planning for the opening of a Women's Center continued in one of the founder's dining room. Start up money of $400 was obtained from the AAUW and community meetings were able to be held monthly (B. Sayre, personal communication, November 10, 1989).

The organization was incorporated as the Women's Center of Eastern Montgomery County. The by-laws describe the purpose of the organization as: a) to apprise people of available resources, services, rights and opportunities; b) to assist women in areas where other resources are not available, such as educating women about their bodies, their physical needs and their rights, teaching women marketable skills, and providing women with telephone and peer counseling and emotional support; and, c) to provide a meeting place for women (Women's Center of Eastern Montgomery County. By-laws, June 13, 1976).

The Early Life of the Organization

The Women's Center was established as a volunteer organization run by an executive board who structure was:

> set up in the form of a coalition or collective similar to the New England Town Meetings. The policy-making is divided among us and each of us is

an equal sponsor of the project. Every woman actively participating in the work of the Center would be a member of the coalition with one vote" (Women's Center of Eastern Montgomery County. Womenews, November, 1975. Available from Women's Center of Montgomery County, The Benson East, Suite B-7, 100 Old York Rd., Jenkintown, PA 19046).

The elected positions of the executive board were Coordinator, Assistant Coordinator, Center Manager, Secretary and Treasurer. The first services were peer groups and a telephone hotline. Eighteen telephone counselors and 12 peer counselors were trained and two consciousness-raising groups and women in transition groups were held. The first Committees concerned women's issues, divorce/widowhood, and abused wives (Women's Center of Eastern Montgomery County. Womenews, November, 1975. Available from Women's Center of Montgomery County, The Benson East, Suite B-7, 100 Old York Rd., Jenkintown, PA 19046).

The Women's Center was located in Abington library, occupying one room large enough to accommodate one telephone counselor. In 1978, the "Eastern" was dropped so that the name of the organization became Women's Center of Montgomery County signifying the organization's representation of the entire area of Montgomery County (B. Sayre, personal communication, November 10, 1989).

The Evolving Organization

In 1979, the organization needed to revise its by-Laws, due to increased membership (over 350 members in 1979). It was felt that a more expedient decision-making process was needed rather than one which, due to lack of attendance, resulted in a wait of one or two months for important decisions to be made. The executive board changed its name to board of directors and the coordinator became president. Robert's Rules of Order were used to conduct meetings (B. Sayre, personal communication, November 10, 1989).

In addition, a full-time Comprehensive Education and Training Act (CETA) employee was hired, along with part-time Title XX employees to perform clerical tasks. In 1980, the Women's Center became a United Way Donor Option agency (Women's Center of Montgomery County. Minutes of Board Meeting, May 13, 1980).

The focus of the organization was domestic violence and the concerns of the Committee On Domestic Violence dominated the board meetings. It was the intention of this group to locate a suitable place to open a domestic violence shelter. A power struggle occurred as this group was making decisions based on their interest in opening a shelter and not in the interests of the Women's Center as a whole. Tensions were high among those women not involved in the shelter opening as well (B. Sayre, personal communication, November 10, 1989).

When the shelter, Laurel House, opened 1980, it was still a part of a Women's Center. However, for the next year, the leaders of Laurel House often made decisions without the total knowledge or acquiescence of the board of Women's Center. Laurel House took over the Women's Center Pennsylvania Coalition Against Domestic Violence membership without notification of the Women's Center's board, while all Women's Center's money was going to support Laurel House. The Women's Center was losing its focus, although the hotline for domestic violence was still located at the Women's Center. The two organizations split at this time, with the Domestic Violence committee leaving the Board of the Women's Center. Laurel House then established its own Board (B. Sayre, personal communication, November 10, 1989). The Women's Center restructured its Board to organize programs under directors.

> The aim is to increase communication among us all and to define and distribute increasing responsibilities" (Women's Center of Montgomery County. Minutes of Board Meeting, September 12, 1981).

In 1983, the organization hired its first paid executive director for the purpose of fundraising. The woman who was hired proposed to raise enough money to pay her salary. (Originally a Woman's Center volunteer, she went to work at another woman's organization before being hired at the Women's Center.) The Women's Center moved to a location where it had to pay rent for the first time. These changes added financial demands, requiring the Executive Director to spend most of her time attracting resources to keep the Women's Center afloat financially. Program expansion became the primary method by which the Women's Center obtained new funding (D. Byrne, personal communication, September 7, 1989).

In 1986, a Norristown branched opened as the Center for the legal advocacy Project. This project provides:

> emotional support, legal options, counseling, and court accompaniment for abused women seeking protection through the courts. We advocate for abused women individually and as a group (Women's Center of Montgomery County. Brochure, undated).

The Women's Center had difficulty getting volunteers to travel to Norristown, so it was felt that opening an office there would encourage volunteerism at the organization. This office is staffed by a full-time project Director. In 1988, a Pottstown office was open for the same purpose. The other new program which is not funded by specific grant or federal funds is the Korean Women's Support Committee. This program started in 1985 by a Korean woman and she has coordinated the program on a volunteer basis since its inception (D. Byrne, personal communication, September 7, 1989).

In 1986, a Norristown branch opened as the center for the legal advocacy project. This project provides:

> emotional support, legal options counseling and court accompaniment for abused women seeking protection through the courts. We advocate for abused women individually and as a group (Women's Center of Montgomery County. Brochure, undated).

The Organization As It Is Today

The Women's Center has increased its paid staff to eight (three full-time and five part-time). This has occurred since 1983, when the only paid staff was the executive. The organization is moving from a volunteer basis to a paid staff. Problems and authority between volunteers and paid staff are occurring. Who directs whom in daily decision-making is the major issue. In some situations, a board member may be giving directions to a paid staff member as director of the area, while the paid staff member directs the board member in the role of volunteer. In addition, it is difficult for paid staff to have influence and authority over a "hard core" of 15 volunteers who have been at Women's Center for many years (D. Byrne, personal communication, September 7, 1989).

The current budget of the Women's Center is $200,000. The funding is evenly divided between governmental (Pennsylvania Coalition Against Domestic Violence) and non-governmental (United Way, private foundations, and membership fees) sources. The rapid expansion of programs housed in different locations has caused a strain on the structural and administrative underpinnings of the organization, as there is limited interaction among the different offices. The Jenkintown office is primarily volunteer-based, while the Norristown office is staff-based. The board of directors and executive director decided jointly that the mission statement would guide problematic decisions (their retention and develop-

ment). Currently, they fill all existing programs are appropriate to the mission statement (D. Byrne, personal communication, September 7, 1989).
The mission statement states:

> The Women's Center of Montgomery County, a feminist community organization, is committed to the goals of helping women and working to effect social change to the betterment of women. The Women's Center of Montgomery County seeks to meet these goals to supportive counseling programs, advocacy programs and educational programs that teach women skills and increase awareness of their rights and opportunities. . . (Women's Center of Montgomery County Mission Statement. <u>Womenews</u>, September, 1989. Available from Women's Center of Montgomery County, The Benson East, Suite B-7, 100 Old York Road, Jenkintown, PA 19046).

The Women's Center has been moving from the grassroots stages to a more professional organization. Volunteers do feel they're losing ownership and that the organization has become more hierarchical. The current structure of the organization is described as an open hierarchy - and which were one person makes the final decisions, yet everyone is open to express their opinion (D. Byrne, personal communication, September 7, 1989).

Major Events In the Organization's Life

1975   First meeting to organize start-up of Women's Center, Incorporated; opened at Abington Library

1978   First paid staff and clerical position

1979   Executive board changed to board of directors; decision-making process change from consensual to by vote

1980   Division within board resulted in the opening Domestic violence shelter - Laurel House

1983   Moved into rent paying situation for first-time; First paid director

1985   Korean Support Group Program (not funded) started

1986   Norristown office, Women's Advocacy Project, opened

1988   Pottstown office, Women's Advocacy Project, opened

1989   Main office moved to larger location in Jenkintown; Executive
        Director and Board decided to emphasize paid staff for provi-
        sion of services and decision-making

The Victim Services Center of Montgomery County
The Birth of the Organization

In 1974, several women who were concerned about issues of rape and
sexual assault and the lack of services to victims of these crimes in Montgomery County began a hotline in the basements of their homes in and
around the Norristown area (Victim Services Center of Montgomery
County. Agency History and Services, undated). These friends established
the service because of their own social consciousness, not as a result of a
personal experience with rape. Initially, they all volunteered their time
and energy with no board of directors or job titles (K. Riccio, personal
communication, November 6, 1989).

Their first decision involved their stance as a feminist organization,
given the political climate of the county. Based on the conservative nature of Montgomery County, and with men holding most positions in the
commissioner's office, the founders decided not to identify themselves
as feminists associated with the radical message which would make it
difficult to obtain money and support from the county commissioners in
fact, there was a conscious effort on the part of the board to screen out the
more radical feminists from becoming associated with the organization.
The issue of rape was presented as mainly affecting women and, thus,
attracted concerned women of broad philosophical persuasion to provide
services to meet the needs of rape or sexual assault victims. This middle-
of-the-road-stance of the founder's enabled the organization to receive
its initial funding from the county commissioner's office and be accepted
and supported by the conservative community in which it was situated
(K. Riccio, personal communication, November 6, 1989).

The Evolving Organization

During the first five years of the organization's existence, there was no formalized training for volunteers. Training instead consisted of experience consciousness-raising experience. For example, one volunteer just completing her volunteer training was sent to a hospital to do crisis intervention, when she just happened to be in the office at the time the call for service came in. Volunteers did whatever was needed at the moment (K. Riccio, personal communication, November 6, 1989).

Volunteer training did become more formalized, as more literature written on the subject and more knowledge was gained. A training manual was the first document developed by the organization.

Sometime between 1977 and 1978, the organization became a United Way-funded organization in the executive director became a full-time staff member (K. Riccio, personal communication, November 6, 1989).

In 1980, several major changes occurred. The Board felt that the organization needed to grow beyond the grassroots stages. In addition, there were opportunities for additional funding and several founders were ready to retire from the organization. At that time, the executive director disagreed with the Board in relation to expanding the purpose of the organization. The executive director began to make unilateral decisions by herself which did not concur with inclinations of the Board and volunteers on the same issue. For example, only two Board members were representatives of the community and had broader perspectives. The Board of volunteer staff felt that, for the survival of the organization, the board membership needed to be expanded to include more community people with diverse professional backgrounds. This was necessary to obtain funding, acceptance and recognition within the community. The executive director opposed opening up the Board representation two additional community people (K. Riccio, personal communication, November 6, 1989).

This disagreement among the Board, the volunteer staff and the executive director precipitated the executive director's resignation. The Board ran the day-to-day operation of the organization until a new executive was chosen. She was selected for her perceived abilities to professionalize the organization and brought several professional staff with her (K. Riccio, personal communication, November 6, 1989).

During this transitional time, the organization changed its name to Rape Crisis Council, Inc., as there were now male volunteers. The board felt that the name change also allow the organization to be more broadly identified by the public, instead of with women exclusively. During the more than three years of this executive directors stay, the organization move to greater professionalism by hiring more paid staff, including a volunteer coordinator. Volunteers no longer did everything but were assigned specific jobs and were supervised by paid professional staff. Volunteers also had less involvement in decision-making, as the volunteer coordinator moved into a decision-making role (K. Riccio, personal communication, November 6, 1989).

The Board deemphasized its previous day-to-day involvement in the organizational operations. For a short time, board members did participate on program committees along with paid staff, but this was not productive for decision-making or the work completion. This organizational form was discontinued shortly after it had begun (K. Riccio, personal communication, November 6, 1989).

The organization suffered another crisis after this executive director left and her successor did not satisfactorily fill the role. After a brief stay with the organization, the successor was fired into money, financial documents and case records with her. The current executive was hired in May 1984 (K. Riccio, personal communication, November 6, 1989).

In August 1985, the organization changed its name from Rape Crisis Center to the Victim Services Center. This name change is representative of the comprehensive victims' services organization now provides. This includes services to a broader victim population: victims of assault, robbery, intimidation, harassment and services to families of homicide victims and male victims (Victim Services Center of Montgomery County. Agency History and Services, undated). The mission of the organization was concomitantly altered from providing services to victims of rape and sexual assaults to victims of serious crimes and their families. Government funding support expanded accordingly (C. Gilhool, personal communication, October 4, 1989).

The Organization As It Is Today

The current executive director has had a major impact on the continuation of the professionalization of the organization. Job positions have become more specialized, with degree requirements attached to them. A policy and procedures manual was written in the organization is now run much like a traditional social service organization. According to the organizational chart of July 1989, the organizational structure is hierarchical, with the project director supervising the four program coordinators. The position of project director adds additional level to the hierarchy and delineate administrative work from direct service. The project director reports directly to the executive director. Decisions are made according to a hierarchical chain of command (C. Gilhool, personal communication, October 4, 1989).

This organization is not a member of the Pennsylvania Coalition Against Rape (PCAR). It does subcontract with PCAR for funds from the State Department of Public Welfare (DPW), which are directed exclusively to the hotline for sexual assault victims and to school programs for the education and prevention of Rape. However, the organization does not identify with the feminist goal of eliminating rape of the Coalition. It does have a strong collaborative relationship with another Montgomery County women's agency, the Women's Center of Montgomery County. Both organizations are in the same building. The Women's Center handles cases of domestic violence in the county and refers rape and sexual assault cases to Victim Service Center. They worked together in order not to duplicate services

The current budget is $289,000 with eight full-time staff and three part-time staff. The annual client direct service statistics for the past three years have shown a consistent pattern of growth. From FY 86/87 to FY 88/89, the number of new clients served has risen from 680 to 1,136, a 67 percent increase. The Prevention Education programs have also increased their services to the community and other professionals such as police. The organization receives more government funding the private or United Way funding. It has a defers funding base, composed of support from many different private foundations, corporations, speaking engagements, memberships, and fund-raising events (Victim Services Center of Montgomery County. '88 Annual Report, 1988).

The number of volunteers has declined in the role that they play within the organization has become more limited. Counseling of victims has become a professional responsibility of paid staff. Volunteers participate and sexual assault counselors, which primarily involves covering hotline, crisis intervention and hospitals, court accompaniment, and speaking engagements.

Major Highlights In the Organization's Life

1974   Hotline began for victims of rape/sexual assault and founders basements

1975   Incorporated as Women Against Rape; founders and a few more original volunteers shared jobs

1976-77 Executive director hired; became U W agency; moved into two-room office

1980   Name changed to Rape Crisis Council; resignation executive director; new executive director hired to professionalize agency

1983-84 Third executive hired in fired due to mishandling of money; operation of agency by Board until current executive hired

1985   Name changed to Victim Services Center to represent a broader victim population

Interim House
The Birth of the Organization

Interim House was conceived of by a woman who was a recovering alcoholic. She was able to convince friends in her neighborhood that there was a need for a halfway house for a recovering alcoholic women in the Germantown area of Philadelphia. In 1971, Interim House was incorporated by 15 founders (eight women and seven men). The first Board of directors meeting was held at a neighborhood church. Many of the original board of directors or individuals affiliated with Eagleville Hospital, a drug and alcohol rehabilitation Hospital in Eagleville, Pennsylvania (Interim House. Minutes of Board Meeting, August 24, 1971).

The Early Life of the Organization

Interim House opened its doors in August 1973 with a grant from the local government agency responsible for funding and monitoring drug and alcohol programs, the Coordinating Office for Drug and Alcohol Abuse Programs (CODAAP), in Philadelphia. The initial grant proposal of November 29, 1972, describes formal job positions which job descriptions attached. The organization did have clearly defined professional job positions such as therapists and social workers. These were written to fit persons chosen for each position by the project director (G. Walters, personal communication, August 17, 1989).

The position of House manager was seen as a key position in working with the women. It was required that the individual filling that position be a recovering alcoholic. The description as stated in the grant proposal, was that:

a house manager must be filled by recovered female with 2 years of sobriety and be a compassionate caring person with a good understanding of Alcoholic Anonymous (Interim House. <u>Grant Proposal to the Coordinating Office for Drug and Alcohol Abuse Programs</u>, August 29, 1972).

The original staff of Interim House did include a male who was the Assistant Director/Clinical Supervisor (a friend of the founder). According to the first house manager, she felt that having a male on staff was a positive aspect for the women living at Interim House, as it helped them to develop appropriate behaviors and relating to men (G. Walters, personal communication, August 17, 1989).

The goals of the organization were to provide a method of service to rehabilitate women alcoholics, to educate the female alcoholic and her family in the prevention and arrest of the disease, and to help the woman to help herself to be independent. The methods by which the goals were obtained included individual and group therapy as well as personal growth courses. The program's focus was on uplifting the self-esteem of the women alcoholics to wait program designed to recognize their uniqueness. AA meetings, psychodramas and role plays were a few of the techniques used (Interim House. <u>Grant Proposal to the Coordinating Office for Drug and Alcohol Abuse Programs</u>, August 29, 1972).

The Evolving Organization

In 1977 CODAAP report documents that Interim House was having both financial and zoning problems. Staff had not received a paycheck in 6 weeks, and a lawsuit had been filed against the organization by a neighbor to prevent the purchase of the home in which the program was operating. The report also stated that there was support documentation of board meetings, few residents from the immediate Philadelphia area, and a critical need for better financial record-keeping. CODAAP's assessment of the situation was that increasing the funding as the director requested was not the answer. CODAAP recommended improved management and control by the director which included better documentation of board meetings and better financial documentation (W. Hicks. Report of the Coordinating Office of Drug and Alcohol Abuse Programs, 1977).

CODAAP required the Director's resignation in 1979 and a female board member took over. However, the financial difficulties as well as leadership problems continue. From 1983 to 1985, three executive directors left (two former board members, one hired from the outside). In 1985, the board agreed to allow CODAAP to contract for outside management for Interim House by Philadelphia Health Management Corp. (PHMC). A project director hired as an employee of PHMC came in to run Interim House. She remained until 1987, when she was replaced by another PHMC female employee (W. Hicks, personal communication, July 26, 1989).

The transition from a "family run" organization to a formal management arrangement with an outside organization created high turnover, whereas previous to this change, although salaries were low, turnover was also low. There is also a change in the racial composition of the staff and executive position. Prior to the "takeover", most of the staff and executive director were black. Since 1985, the director, whose title changed at that time the project director as part of the PHMC organizational structure, is white (W. Hicks, personal communication, July 26, 1989).

In 1984, the facility change locations to its current location where there have not been any major neighbor problems. It expanded its funding to include United Way monies in 1986 for special programs for the women. An operations manual as well as a policy manual were prepared in 1985 by the PHMC management where previously in informal system had existed (R. Hornstein, personal communication, July 21, 1989).

The Organization As It Is Today

After 4 years of management by PHMC, as was agreed when the outside management contract was initiated with CODAAP, PHMC took over control of Interim House in 1989. The Board of Directors has now been dissolved and a new Board of Directors is being constituted. There are currently five Directors on the Board, one of whom is an original founding member of Interim House (W. Hicks, personal communication, July 26, 1989). The current project director is leaving in August, 1989 to return school and the organization will be without a project director (R. Hornstein, personal communication, July 21, 1989).

The current budget of Interim House is $400,000. The organization continues to receive the bulk of its funding from CODAAP, with a small yearly grant from United Way ($18,000) and, for the first time this current fiscal year, a small grant of $1,500 from Women's Way (R. Hornstein, personal communication, July 21, 1989).

The facility houses 22 women for up to six months. The women residents are required to pay rent from their welfare checks and Exchange their food stamps for their food. There are 11 employees, seven full-time and three part-time, and no volunteer staff. All the therapists have advanced professional degrees (R. Hornstein, personal communication, July 21, 1989).

The original mission of the organization has expanded to include help for women and recovery from abuse of other substances. In the Policy and Procedures Manual of 1985 prepared by PHMC, the goals of the organization are:

> To facilitate the resident's acceptance of herself as addicted to alcohol and/or other substances and inculcate the goal of abstinence; to provide a therapeutic milieu in which to conduct an effective residential recovery and rehabilitation program for women who are substance abusers; to help substance abusers to identify and use alternative methods of dealing with negative emotional responses to stress in place of using a substance . . . and to enable women to experience their female identity as a source of pride . . . (Interim House. Policy and Procedures Manual, 1985).

In addition, there is an attempt on current management's part to offer a new outpatient therapy program (R. Hornstein, personal communication, July 21, 1989).

The operation of the Interim House has become very formalized, professional and specialized. A comptroller is a new adjunct job position shown on the organizational chart developed by PHMC. (Interim House. Policy and Procedures Manual, 1985).

Major Highlights In the Organization's Life

1971   Incorporated as Interim House

1973   Open doors at first location as halfway house for recovering women alcoholics

1977   Financial and zoning problems highlighted by funding report

1979   Founder resigns, Board member takes over as Director

1983-85 Succession of three directors

1984   Moves to a new location (bigger house with no neighbor problems)

1985   Agreement with funding source suggestion to retain outside management; informal arrangement between funding source and Management Corporation to manage Interim House for 4 years

1987   New project director hired by PHMC agency (outside managers)

1989   Takeover completed by outside management organization, as per agreement with CODAAP; board dissolves with new board information; current director expected to leave in August, 1989

Philadelphia Women's Network
The Birth of the Organization

The impetus for the founding of the Philadelphia Women's Network was the 1978 meeting of two of the founders as a result of the collaboration of their business corporations on a grant proposal. Both women were in the upper-management levels of large male-dominated corporations. During the writing of the proposal, which they worked on together, the two women discovered that they had some similar concerns in their roles in management of large corporations. They decided to ask other women they each knew to come together to provide support for each other and to share their experiences as upper of level managers (M. Brown personal communication, December 16, 1989).

In June of 1978, ten women met in a conference room of one of their corporations after work hours. They form the nucleus of the Philadelphia Business Network. A larger meeting was planned so that they could attract other Philadelphia career women working in a variety of fields. They wanted to develop a network of friends from different areas of expertise to contact when they want advice and support for their own daily career concerns. They booked a room at a local hotel and sent out invitations to women on lists of business women from a variety of sources. Funding for this first event came from the founders themselves (M. Brown, personal communication, December 16, 1989). The first membership meeting was held in November, 1978. The attendance exceeded their expectations. More than 100 women attended, many of whom had not met each other before (M. Brown personal communication, December 16, 1989).

The Early Life of the Organization

The organization was run by the original founders, who were the elected officers of the board of directors. Each founder participated in the writing of the organization's purpose:

> To promote a spirit of cooperation and understanding among its members; to enhance members ' professional contacts, opportunities for expanded learning and mutual support and encouragement; to achieve recognition of the contribution of women to the Philadelphia community; and to the courage other women to seek professional positions within the Philadelphia community (Philadelphia Women's Network. PWN Brochure, undated).

By 1980, all the founders had rotated off the board but remained active as members of the organization. In the early days, there were 250 members (M. Brown personal communication, December 16, 1989).

Members of the organization were entitled to: program activities including dinner meetings with guest speakers on current issues and on a wide range of topics of interest to career women; social gatherings/events; small group discussions of topics of mutual concern; seminars and workshops conducted by experts; and monthly newsletter; and membership directory; and an annual report. The membership dues were $55 (Philadelphia Business Network. PWN Brochure, undated). In order to become a member, a woman had to complete a membership application, which included eligibility requirements such as having two Philadelphia Women's Network sponsors, extensive business experience, or advanced degree with business experience and organizational and professional affiliations (Philadelphia Women's Network. Application for Membership, undated).

The Evolving Organization

The organization hired a part-time administrative assistant to perform clerical tasks and to send out mailings. The other work of the organization was done by the Board and members. Committees continued to be the means by which the members planned and participated in the organization's operation. Meetings occurred once a month, with fees charged for each event. Members receive a reduced rate for events. Events were open to non-members at a higher fee. Men were welcome at the meetings and there were no stipulations that men cannot join the network but men have never joined (N. Pigford, personal communication, September 18, 1989).

The organization dropped its membership eligibility requirements of to Philadelphia Women's Network sponsors by applicants and stream-lined its application process.

The Organization As It Is Today

Currently, a $10 application fee is charged. Membership fees are cur-rently $75. The original membership application form has been incorpo-rated as a tear-off portion of the organization's brochure (Philadelphia Women's Network. PWN Brochure, undated).

Philadelphia Women's Network has moved to offer services to women outside the organization. Approximately a year-and-a-half ago, the Board approved a mentoring program. The organization had reached a point of maturity which enabled the members to think about giving back to oth-ers, specifically, to young professional women who are just starting out in their careers. Beginning as a task force which evolved into a commit-tee, a program was developed in which members were recruited to serve as mentors to women who are "newcomers" in the business world. The first class began in January of 1989 and in September of that year, they were honored as graduates. A new class of "newcomers" will begin in January, 1990 (N. Pigford, personal communication, September 18, 1989).

Enhancing the networks presence in the community and building PWN membership are two vital goals for the coming year. The current budget is about $20,000. It is felt that membership has declined due to more competition from other business-related women's groups, such as the Forum for Executive Women. One of the problems contributing to low membership is the generic nature of the organization as opposed to orga-nizations that are specific to saleswomen, executives, or specific profes-sions. Philadelphia Women's Network does work in cooperation with other Women's Business networks. The organization is a member of the International Alliance and has informal relations with other women's busi-ness organizations, such as the National Association of Women's Busi-ness Organizations (N. Pigford, personal communication, September 18, 1989).

The only paid staff in the organization is an administrative assistant. Turnover has been very low in this position, with two people occupying it. The Board of Directors are the power in the organization and the decision-making body. They vote on all major decisions, such as new initiatives, but on less crucial issues, such as the type of programs offered during the course of the year, the program chair is given the authority for her group to decide, usually based on group consensus (N. Pigford, personal communication, September 18, 1989).

Major Highlights In the Organization's Life

1978   Founding of PWN by 10 women in middle to upper management and large corporations

1980   Original Board members rotated off Board, but remained active as members, membership eligibility requirements of to sponsors dropped

1984   Membership in The International Alliance, an international umbrella organization of women's professional groups

1988   Taskforce organized to develop for services to women outside the organization, the mentoring program

1989   Graduation the first group of "newcomers"

Women In Transition
The Birth of the Organization

Women In Transition (WIT) grew out of a volunteer hotline at the Women's Liberation Center in West Philadelphia. Telephone calls were primarily from women undergoing separation or divorce. With the staff of two and $20,000 in funding from churches and private foundations, the two founders formed an organization addressing the needs of separating and divorcing women. The organization incorporated in 1972, providing a hotline and peer support groups similar to the consciousness-raising groups of Women's Liberation Center for to women going through the transitions of separation and divorce (McMahon, undated).

The Early Life of the Organization

The founders were dedicated to a collective model of decision-making. There were no personnel policies, no titles, no job descriptions, and everyone received the same salary. The members of the organization shared all jobs, doing whatever was needed at any given time. There were no volunteers, as the founders believed that women should be paid for their work. During the first year, funding was uncertain and, at times, paychecks were late or were not received. Several organization members went on unemployment when money was very tight (McMahon, undated). The purpose of the organization was to:

> develop a multi-faceted program geared towards promoting the economical and emotional independence and well-being of women and children in need to a broad based program providing a variety of services (Women in Transition. Articles of Incorporation, September 25, 1972).

Out of this purpose developed a structured peer support group model for separating and divorcing women; survival skills workshops in low-income housing projects; the training program for mental health workers; and a publishing and book on separation and divorce which was and still is distributed nationally (McMahon, undated).

In 1975, WIT's founding members decided to accept funding from the local Community Mental Health Center to provide counseling services within the center's jurisdiction. Although the organization retained its own identity, it did receive what founding members considered "tainted" funds. These funds had strings attached in relation to expectations of formalization and changes in the current organizational structure (Galper and Washbourne, 1976).

In 1976, WIT began a wife abuse program, becoming a founder of the Pennsylvania Coalition Against Domestic Violence. The focus on domestic violence information and referral services has remained as one of the organization's major foci (S. L. McMahon, personal communication, August 3, 1989).

Internal conflict emerged as WIT's status grew in the community and the number of women participating in the collective increased. With seven women as collective members, the collective model of decision-making left the staff vulnerable to power plays and disagreements on issues. With the help of an outside consultant, the organization members agreed to a co-director model with an advisory board of directors (McMahon, undated).

The Evolving Organization

WIT went through an expansion period during its first 10 years. In 1980, with a loss of major government funding, WIT experienced a financial crisis which necessitated several major changes. At that time, the organization resigned from Women's Way, the funding coalition for women's organizations, in order to join the United Way. One of the co-directors left and the other co-director became executive director. A Board of Directors was established. Layoffs of recently trained WIT staff occurred and morale among the remaining WIT staff was poor (S. L. McMahon, personal communication, August 3, 1989).

The Board of Directors and Executive Director develop a strategic plan to expand funding sources and to develop new programs. One new program, different from any previous WIT program, was the OASIS program of outreach, assessment, advocacy and referral of addicted women. This was funded in 1985 by the local coordinating office of drug and alcohol programs, the Coordinating Office of Drug and Alcohol Abuse Programs (CODAAP). A conflict developed between the Women of WIT who subscribed to a feminist empowerment counseling model and the recovering women who subscribed to the confronted treatment model utilized by addiction counselors. Complaints of discrimination were received by the funding source from the OASIS "outside" staff against the WIT staff. The organization almost lost this program, but was able to negotiate a resolution through a staff communication-building process facilitated by outside consultants. It was deemed necessary for the managers to take on greater authoritative roles in order to clarify responsibilities. This led to the resignations of old-timers, who had difficulty integrating this model with the former collective model of decision-making. Included in the resignations was that of the Executive Director in 1988 (McMahon, undated).

The Organization As It Is Today

The current executive was already a staff member with several years of tenure with the organization. In addition, she has been active in the Philadelphia feminist community for more than ten years. She is focusing on stabilizing the organization, with its many diverse programs ranging from the substance abuse OASIS program to domestic violence information and referral. The program emphasis has shifted from domestic violence to drug and alcohol rehabilitation services. The professionals who have come into the organization have been integrated into the structure by the continued development of a hierarchical structure. The current Executive Director has emphasized task rather than process (R. Hacker, personal communication, September 29, 1989).

The annual budget three is currently $450,000. Their eight paid full-time staff, six paid part-time staff and 15 consultants. The organization does utilize volunteers for its hotline (R. Hacker, personal communication, September 29, 1989). Funding is received from diverse sources, which include equal portions from government and private funding sources. In addition, membership fees and fees for services are received. The organization struggles financially, with expenses exceeding revenues for this current fiscal year (R. Hacker, personal communication, September 29, 1989).

Major Highlights In the Organization's Life

1971 Founded as Women In Transition to provide hotline services and group support to separating in divorcing women; operated as collective

1972 Incorporated

1974 Accepted first government money which stabilize programs; moved to co-director model

1975-80 Experienced growth. With much reliance on government funding; founder of PCADV

1980 Lost major government funding; resignation of one co-director; other became sole executive director; left Women's Way to affiliate with United Way; establishment of Board of Directors

1980-88 Variety of new programs initiated, with one program (OASIS) moving WIT beyond original purpose to drug and alcohol service; resignation of Executive director

1988 current executive is promoted from within; fee for service established

Women Organized Against Rape
The Birth of the Organization

In 1972, the issue of rape was receiving much attention in Philadelphia due to a rash of rape occurring in and around the city. One woman, who had shared the pain of a friend who had not only been brutally raped but had endured humiliation in the hospital from police and courts, decided to speak out for action (Women Organized Against Rape. Background And History of Women Organized Against Rape, 1989).

On the 52nd anniversary of the 19th Amendment granting women the right to vote, 300 women marched in Philadelphia to protest their dissatisfaction with the progress of women's rights. The founder of Women Organized Against Rape (WOAR), Jody Pinto, spoke out about rape at that gathering. As a result of her speech, a planning committee evolved to begin the process of organizing against rape (Women Organized Against Rape. Background and History of Women Organized Against Rape, 1989).

On May 1, 1973, after almost a year of planning, Women Against Rape (WOAR) announced the opening of its rape crisis center in a small room at Philadelphia General Hospital (PGH). Twenty volunteers and no paid staff members became emergency room companions to rape victims when the arrived at PGH and provided crisis counseling to victims, their families, and friends over WOAR 24-hour hotline (Women Organized Against Rape. Background and History of Women Organized Against Rape, 1989).

The goals of WOAR as stated in their 1972 by-laws were: to eliminate rape in our society, beginning with the community that WOAR serves; to provide needed support and referrals to victims of rape, their families, and friends in Philadelphia; and, to empower women to gain control over their lives (Women Organized Against Rape. By-laws, 1972).

The Early Life of the Organization

WOAR was run by a ten member steering committee. There were two co-chairwomen and seven other committees, each with a committee leader. In 1974, WOAR presented formal proposals to the mayor, the District Attorney, and the Police Commissioner aimed at increasing rape reporting and enhancing rape awareness in the criminal justice system. The court companion program began with WOAR establishing a desk in both City Hall and Family Court to be more accessible to victims during court proceedings (Women Organized Against Rape. Background and History of Women Organized Against Rape, 1989).

By the summer of 1974, Jody Pinto had left the organization and returned to painting. She felt that her skills were in organizing, not in operating the organization on a day-to-day basis. She had laid a strong foundation by choosing women who were experts in the areas needed to develop a growing program (J. Pinto, personal communication, November 18, 1989). However, her strong leadership was missed and later that year, other original members also left en mass. In 1975, WOAR hired its first paid director and five other full-time staff members to help run the organization. In 1976, a board of directors was established to replace the steering committee. The decision-making process was changed from the whole membership voting on each decision to only elected officers voting on decisions. This change enabled decisions to be made faster (B. Simon, personal communication, November 18, 1989).

During the period of 1974 to 1976, WOAR was actively establishing relationships with the legal and medical systems. WOAR's proposals to the district attorney's office were implemented. When PGH closed, WOAR was instrumental in assuring continuity of care of rape victims and conducted training sessions in rape awareness for hospital staffs of the two hospitals selected to treat victims. In addition, WOAR members advocated for rape legislation and participated in the formation of the Pennsylvania Coalition Against Rape (Women Organized Against Rape. Background and History of Women Organized Against Rape, 1989).

The Evolving Organization

In 1980, WOAR's child sexual abuse program began. Work with sexually abused children became a major new dimension of the organization (Simon, 1982). The organization had three directors, each for a 2 year period of time, between 1975 and 1980. The first director was considered to be a strong administrator who established systematic procedures for staff operations. This director was forced by the staff to resign because of her domination. The next director was forced to resign by the volunteers who constituted the elected board of directors due to her lack of administrative skills. The third director was considered to have maintained an expanded the daily routines and systems while providing positive leadership (Simon, 1982).

In 1981, the membership voted to stop referring to WOAR as a volunteer organization. The organization had twelve paid staff members. A substantial amount of the work in direct service and education/training as well as most of the advocacy work was done by staff (Women Organized Against Rape. The Work of Women Organized Against Rape, 1981).

WOAR continued its advocacy work to improve treatment and benefits of sexual assault victims. WOAR also spoke out against Philadelphia judges' decisions on rape cases and offensive remarks about rape victims. WOAR was successful in getting action against these judges' behavior. With government funding, WOAR hired a case manager for children and adolescents and clinical director to enhance its short-term counseling alternatives for victims of sexual assault and their families (Women Organized Against Rape. Background and History of Women Organized Against Rape, 1989).

The Organization As It Is Today

The current Executive Director has been with the organization since 1980. She has been Executive Director since 1985. One of her goals has been to increase the decision-making power of the executive director; she found that when she first became the Executive, the decision-making process was very slow due to an inexperienced Board of Directors who asked lots of questions while making few decisions (K, Kulp, personal communication, August 29, 1989).

A new brochure titled "Sexual Assault and Aids" published in 1989, is the new focus for public information distribution by WOAR. Another new educational program instituted in 1989 is WOAR's work with rape crisis centers across the state to develop a curriculum for junior high school students challenging sexual stereotypes (Women Organized Against Rape. WOARPATH, Summer 1989. Available from WOAR, 125 South 9th Street, Suite 601, Philadelphia, PA 19107). In 1989, WOAR has sponsored a conference on teens and sexual violence for professionals working with adolescents and a "national coalition against sexual assault" conference. Its clinical counseling program is professionally staffed, with no volunteers providing counseling and ongoing support groups for adult and adolescent rape and incest survivors (Women Organized Against Rape. WOARPATH, Summer 1989. Available from WOAR, 125 South 9th Street, Suite 601, Philadelphia, PA 19107).

Although there are currently over 100 volunteers, according to the current executive director, recruitment of minorities for volunteer work is a goal. The organization now receives more than 2/3 of its funding from government sources. The annual budget s $729,000. There are 24 paid professional staff with only three clerical staff. Since 1986, the work with children who are survivors of sexual assault and incest has been integrated into the adult programs of the organization. The newest program still in the planning stages is the Training and Research Institute. This proposal for start-up funding addresses sexual assault issues by expanding training and education within the context of clinical services. It is conceived by WOAR that the Training and Research Institute will be a satellite office reaching out to minorities dealing with the issues of substance abuse, AIDS and sexual assault (K. Kulp, personal communication, August 29, 1989).

Major Highlights in the Organization's Life

1972   Founder of WOAR spoke out at the 52nd anniversary of the 19th Amendment to bring attention to the issue of rape

1973   After a year of planning WOAR announced the opening of its rape crisis center at Philadelphia General Hospital; the first services were crisis counseling and a 24-hour hotline

1974   Founder left to return to art; WOAR experienced leadership problems; legislative proposals to city government receive support

1975   Representative of WOAR participated in the formation of the Pennsylvania Coalition Against Rape; successor to founder hired; WOAR established a board of directors out of the steering committee; elected officers replace voting by all members

1980   WOAR's child sexual abuse program began; emergency room crisis counseling moved to a different hospital requiring WOAR train hospital personnel on sensitivity issues related to rape victims

1985   Current Executive Director begins reign

1989   New public information focus on sexual assault and AIDS; plans underway for Training and Research Institute targeting a minority area for preventative clinical services; executive director now has more decision-making power than previous slower process of board involvement in all decisions

The Women's Therapy Center
The Birth of the Organization

The original name of this organization was the Feminist Therapy Collective, founded by eight women in 1972. The founders of the organization came together from two sources: (a) from a group of women psychologists who attend a consciousness-raising group at Temple University, which focused on clinical and research issues of alienation in women, an (b) attendees at a Women In Transition (WIT) training workshop for volunteer group facilitators for WIT support groups. One of the women who attended the WIT session wrote down her fantasy of wanting to start a feminist therapy center and another woman acted upon it by gathering together eight women psychologist and social workers from the above two groups interested in providing feminist psychotherapy (S. Elias, personal communication, September 19, 1989).

The Early Life of the Organization

The organization was initiated with the donation of $200 from each founder which enabled them to rent space in a rowhouse in Center City. All of the founders worked at the Feminist Therapy Collective part-time, as they were either in school or held other full-time positions. There were no paid salaries. By the time of incorporation in 1974, all therapists received pay of $2.00 an hour. Client fees were the sole source of revenue and were based on a sliding fee scale which started at zero. It was the intention of the Center not to turn away anyone, so scholarships were available, but women were asked to contribute $2.00 per session as a commitment to their own growth. The first services provided were individual and group therapy, with the emphasis on developing a feminist group therapy model. The model was built on the empowerment, support and definition of life choices for women (Elias, S. The Feminist Therapy Collective. Paper presented at Bryn Mawr Graduate School of Social Work and Social Research, Bryn Mawr, PA, November, 1972).

The Articles of Incorporation identify the purposes of the organization as: 1) providing individual and group therapy services to persons in order to promote their growth a responsible, autonomous individuals who are able to choose and create options for living which transcend the cultural norms and boundaries of sex; 2) providing mental health services to women (direct clinical services); and, 3) providing services to men and children in the context of couple and family therapy (The Feminist Therapy Collective. Articles of Incorporation, March, 1974).

In 1974, the Feminist Therapy Collective hired a coordinator to do the jobs they formerly shared, which were necessary to the maintenance of the collective. This position was designed for a doctoral student competent to handle emergency clinical issues but who could not vote on policy (P. Mikols, personal communication, September 6, 1989).

The founders modeled the collective structure of the organization after the Berkeley Radical Therapy model, used by the Boston Women's Health Center. The decision-making process involved all members who made decisions as a group based on principles of feminism and collective operation. The Feminist Therapy Collective was the first collective to offer individual and group psychotherapy to women on a continuing basis. As a collective, the organization members worked together on an equal, non-hierarchical basis. There were two positions, that of secretary and treasurer which rotated). They were not paid positions. The Feminist Therapy Collective remained a collective without a Board of Directors until 1984 (P. Mikols, personal communication, September 6, 1989).

The Evolving Organization

The organization lacked consistent procedures and policies. There were no written manuals. Instead, the members of the collective concentrated on writing position papers on feminist therapy, such as Feminist Therapy: A Working Definition (1977).

In 1982, the Empowerment Quarterly, a newsletter to members, came out for a brief period of time. Although announcements were sent out to local college newspapers, most referrals came from other clients. Emphasis was placed on use of quality, professionally trained therapists, who had, at minimum, a graduate degree. Doctorates in related field were actually the rule for the therapists. Outside supervision was encouraged (P. Mikols, personal communication, September 6, 1989).

During the first 8 years of its organizational life, there was constant turnover of collective members (therapists). One of the original founders left in 1974 to go into private practice. The organization was used as a stepping stone into private practice by many of the founders and subsequent therapists. When therapists left, they would often take their clients with them (S. Elias, personal communication, September 19, 1989).

By 1980, financial stress became a major issue for organization members. One of the original founders wrote a letter to a Task Force organized to look into the financial difficulties of the collective. The problems within the organization were stated in her letter as: 1) existence largely to satisfy the needs of the member; 2) dysfunctional decision-making process and follow-through 3) fear of outside influences; 4) inability to delegate power and responsibility effectively; 5) constantly changing rules; 6) devaluing of emerging leaders and, 7) lack of long range fiscal planning (D.

Chambless. <u>Letters to the Feminist Therapy Collective Task Force</u>, December 21, 1980).

Along with an outside consultant, the Task Force decided that, because there was a need for direction and leadership, both short-term and long-term, the organization should transform into a more traditional management structure governed by a working Board of Directors as the policy-making body of the agency. In 1982, the first Board of Directors was formed. In addition, the organization changed its name to the Women's Therapy Center to more accurately represent the organization's services to all women who are seeking therapy (The Feminist Therapy Collective. <u>Report of the Task Force</u>, July 15, 1982). The change in name was not an easy one and at least one document illustrates continued use of the name, "Feminist Therapy Collective" intermixed with "Women's Therapy Center" for several years after the name change (The Feminist Therapy Collective. <u>FTC Constitution</u>, November, 1984).

Since 1984, Board members have been elected and are not current members of the staff. 1984, a Constitution was written, which includes a mission statement. The mission statement describes the organization as a

> Private non profit mental health center for women. Our purpose is to promote growth of women as responsible, autonomous individuals who are able to choose and create lie options that transcend role expectations based solely on gender through counseling and psychotherapy, referral and information giving, education, outreach advocacy and professional training, the organization meets the mental health needs of women (The Feminist Therapy Collective. <u>FTC Constitution</u>, November, 1984).

Also included in the Constitution is the agency's commitment to alternative functioning. It is functionally alternative because of the nature of the methods employed: to communicate to all members; to share and provide access to information; to allow for input in the decision-making process and document dissenting opinions; and, to make decisions by majority vote (The Feminist Therapy Collective. <u>FTC Constitution</u>, November, 1984).

The Organization As It Is Today

The Women's Therapy Center has institutionalized its new name and policies and procedures. In 1987, a logo was designed for use with the new name and, in 1989, a new brochure was developed, which is now being distributed. From 1984 on, the Board's efforts have been concentrated on formalizing the procedures and policies of the organization. Each therapist signs a contract which contains illness and vacation policies and job descriptions and requirements. More administrative staff, such as clinical coordinator, have been hired and the sliding fee scale has been changed to a minimum of $25.00 per session. Outside funding, such as foundation money, has been sought and the organization has become a United Way Donor Option recipient (in 1987). The current budget is $100,000 (J. Biordi, personal communication, August 9, 1989).

All of the employees of the organization work part-time, and in 1986, for insurance purposes, their status changed from employee to fee-for-service. Part-time therapist must carry their own malpractice insurance. The administrative coordinator acts as a liaison between the Board and staff. In 1984, an organizational chart was designed to include an executive director, but this position has never been filled. The administrative assistant and the clinical coordinator work together and function as an executive. There are no current plans to hire an executive. The current emphasis of the organization is on re-establishing the breadth of the programs offered in the early days. Group workshops are a developing function. The current Boar is moving from a working Board to a fundraising Board. The thrust for the organization leaders is toward maintaining visibility in the form of an agency, not as a private practice model, and creating a structure that encourages the togetherness that existed within the Collective, but was lost when the organization transformed to the Board of Directors model. Group supervision is provided by the clinical coordinator and the administrative coordinator concentrates on standardizing agency procedures, such as interviewing all referrals in person (J. Biordi, personal communication, August 9, 1989).

Major Highlights In the Organization's Life

1972   Service initiated

1974   Incorporated as The Feminist Therapy Collective, Inc.

1980   Task Force to study financial crisis; Letter from one of the founders to the Task Force identified problems of the organization

1981   First Board of Directors established; Name changed to The Women's Therapy Center; Large turnover of therapists

1984-86 Constitution written; Transition to new name

1987-89 Affiliation with United Way; Administrator hired and Clinical coordinator hired; Move to agency model from private practice model

Conclusion

Table 4.1 is a compilation of demographics of the 15 organizations studied. In this study there are four organizations serving victims of domestic violence. All of the four domestic violence organizations provide hotline and counseling services. In addition, two of the four organizations also operate shelters. There were also four organizations providing services to victims of sexual assault and rape. Two of these four organizations serve victims of sexual assault exclusively while the other two have evolved into comprehensive crime victims serving all victim of all violent crimes. One of the two substance abuse organizations in this study is a residential program while the other is a group self-help program. The two health care organizations in this study, an abortion clinic and a birthing center, were founded by the same woman. And finally, there is one career/employment support organization, one mental health organization and one information and referral organization in this study.

The 15 organizations studied range in age from 10 years (two organizations) to 18 years (one organization). Five of the 15 organizations studied are 16 years old. The annual budget of the 15 organizations range from $25,000 to $800,000. Four organizations have annual budgets of $100,000 or less, while, at the other extreme, two organizations have annual budgets of over $700,000. Four of the organizations studied have annual budgets between $400,000 and $600,000.

Total number of paid staff ranges from one in two organizations to 20 or more in three organizations. As expected, those organizations with larger budgets have more paid employees. One organization utilizes only part-time paid staff. Ten of the 15 organizations currently have a strong volunteer component with numbers of volunteers ranging from 20 to over 100. Nine of the 15 organizations receive the majority of their funding from government funding sources. Two of the 15 organizations receive funding from membership fees only. The other four receive a combination of private foundation monies, United Way money, and membership fees.

Type of Organization			Age of Organization			Amount of Annual Budget (In Thousands)		
Domestic Violence	=	4	18 years	=	1			
Sexual Assault	=	2	17 years	=	1	700-800	=	2
Victim Services Center	=	2	16 years	=	5	400-600	=	4
Substance Abuse	=	2	15 years	=	2	200-400	=	5
Health Care	=	2	14 years	=	1	100	=	2
Career/Employment	=	1				under 100	=	2
Information and Referral	=	1						
Mental Health	=	1						

Range of Number Of Paid Staff			County of Organization		
+20	=	3	Bucks	=	2
+15	=	2	Chester	=	2
10-15	=	4	Delaware	=	3
under 10	=	6	Montgomery	=	3
			Philadelphia	=	5

Table 4.1
Demographics of the 15 Organizations Studied

Chapter Five

Data Analysis

Introduction

This section presents an aggregated descriptive analysis of change, if any, along the six dimensions (goals, formalization, authority structure, division of labor, personal relationships, and reward system) of the 15 organization studied. The six dimensions were selected for their ability to capture the difference between alternative feminist and traditional bureaucratic organizations. Data were collected on each of these six dimensions at two points in time, year one and the current year. Data sources were documentation made available to the researcher by the current leader of each organization and interviews conducted by the research with original organizational members and current leaders.

The literature (Galper and Washburne, 1976; McShane and Oliver, 1978; Johnson, 1981; Riger, 1984) and the pilot study have identified a characteristic emphasis on social change goals in feminist organizations at the initial stage of development. In order to describe over time, what, if any, change in goal emphasis occurred, data documenting type of goals were collected for each organization at the two points in time. Interviewees were questioned as to the goal emphasis of the organization at these two points in time.

The dimension of formalization describes the degree of formal documentation in the areas of communication, procedures, and rules in feminist organizations (Riger, 1984). Data were collected on the existence of personnel manuals, procedure manuals, job descriptions, organizational charts, minutes of staff meetings and the organization pamphlets and brochures at two points in time, year one and the current year, in order to capture change in the degree of formalization of the organization. Interviewees were questioned regarding the extent of distribution of these documents to organization members at the two points studied.

The literature (McShane and Oliver, 1978; Riger, 1984; Valentich and Gripton, 1984) and the pilot study identified the importance of founders' personal relationships, often developed out of attendance at consciousness-raising (C-R) groups, as providing the impetus to establish organizations to address issues raised in such groups. In order to describe what, if any, change occurred over time in the importance of personal relationships in feminist organizations, data were collected on this variable as documented in job descriptions from year one and the current year. In addition, founders and current organization leaders were interviewed regarding the extent to which organization members knew each other through affiliations and activities with other feminist organizations prior to employment at the organization in question.

Purposive and friendship rewards have been identified as initially more important than material rewards for individuals working in feminist organizations (Rothschild-Whitt, 1976; Riger, 1984). Change over time in emphasis on non-material versus material rewards was captured by data collected on the relative emphasis on material and non-material rewards as well as on the existence of differential staff remuneration at year one and the current year. Interviewees were questioned regarding the longevity of organizational affiliation and the level of competitiveness of the organization's salaries in comparison to other similar organizations in the community for the two time points under study.

According to prior research, feminist organizations have few specialized job positions requiring technical qualifications at the initial stage of development (Riger, 1984) and evidence minimal division of labor (Rothschild-Whitt, 1976). In order to describe what change occurred in the level of job specialization in the feminist organizations studied here, data were collected on the documented existence of discrete job positions for year one and the current year. Interviewees were questioned as to how the work was divided, including any existing job rotation among organization members.

Both the literature reviewed (Galper and Washburne, 1976; McShane and Oliver, 1981; Riger, 1984) and the pilot study have identified a concern in feminist organizations for distributing power equally through a collective organizational structure as opposed to the hierarchical structure of traditional organizations. Change over time in authority structure from a collective, egalitarian structure to a bureaucratic, traditional authority structure is described by data collected on the existence of hierarchical levels at two points in time in the organizations studied here. Interview respondents were asked about staff participation in the decision-making process at the two points in time, year one and the present.

Descriptive Analysis
Goals

Goals are the general purposes of an organization as put forth in its charter, annual reports, public statements by key executives, and other authoritative pronouncements (Hall, 1972). Riger (1984) identifies the goal orientation of "Feminist Movement Organizations (FMOs)" as ranging

From being remedial in nature, aiming to reduce the impact of the problem once it has occurred and adopting individuals as the target of change efforts, to being concerned with primary prevention and aiming at change in institutions and society (p. 106).

Documentation exists which presents each organizations initial goals for the 15 organization in this study. These stated goals have been designated as either client service or social change goals. Client service goals make statements abut promoting the welfare of women by addressing their needs through service activities (Riger, 1984). The goals of the rape crisis centers in this study of providing services to rape victims are examples of client service goal statements. Social change goals make statements about promoting the welfare of women by addressing their needs through social and political activities. The goal of Women Organized Against Rape, (WOAR), found in the organization's 1976 By-Laws, of "eliminating rape in our society beginning with the community WOAR serves" is one example of a social change goal statement. These client service and/or social change goals inform the organizations' mission statements, statement of purpose, philosophy statements, and articles of incorporation.

A count of the number of each goal type stated in the organizations' earliest documentation, including articles of incorporation, mission statements, brochures, found that all fifteen organizations had client service goals at inception. In addition, eight of the 15 organizations presented social change goals in their earliest documents. These eight organizations are: A Woman's Place, Domestic Abuse Project, Women Against Rape, Women's Resource Center, Women's Center of Montgomery County, Women In Transition, Women Organized Against Rape and Women's Therapy Center. One organization, Women's Suburban Clinic, did not document its social change goal until 1987 in its feminist philosophy statement, but according to its founder, Sherely Hollos, advocating for reproductive rights has always been an organizational goal (S. Hollow, personal communication, August 2, 1989).

Weiner (1982) defines a goal statement as

A policy statement that generally leads to the development of one or more programs (set of activities) that collectively will contribute to the reduction/elimination of the problem identified by the policy (p. 225).

According to Weisbord (1976), a goal statement combines the influence of the environment (what we have to do for society to support us) and the influence of the founders (what we want to do). "The outcome of this negotiation is called 'priorities'. Priorities are translated into programs..." (Weisbord, 1976, p. 18).

The social change goals of these eight organization influenced organizational activity. At inception, the presence of social change goals in these organizations was associated with providing education services and training to the general public as well as to social systems (legal, medical, social and political). For example, one of the first tasks of the founders of Women Against Rape and A Woman's Place was to provide sensitivity training to police officers working with victims of rape and domestic violence, respectively. In addition, the domestic violence organizations and the rape crisis organizations formed state-wide coalitions (Pennsylvania Coalition Against Domestic Violence and Pennsylvania Coalition Against Rape) which advocated at the state level for funding as well as influenced governmental policy decisions affecting victims of sexual assault or rape and domestic violence.

As Rothschild and Whitt (2986) state,

> Alternative enterprises do best when they are able to ferret out a market that mainstream organizations cannot or will not enter because the product requires handmade or custom production, because public agencies fail to provide a required service... (p. 116).

The client services provided by the 15 organizations studied were not provided by existing public and private agencies. For example, there were no existing services specifically for sexual assault/rape victims, victims of domestic violence, abortions, birthing centers, career support groups or drug and alcohol programs specifically for women.

From client service goals, new service models were developed to address the unmet needs of women (Powell, 1986). For example, the Women's Resource Center identified the unmet need of the women who attended an open meeting to discuss the possibility of developing a women's center. These unmet needs include a place to meet, an information and referral system, and workshops and groups. Concrete services were provided in the form of a systematized information and referral hotline, as well as workshops and support groups on issues identified by the women who came to the newly created women's center (Hopkins, undated). Programs, developed out of client service goals, were specific to the issues the organizations were conceived to address. For instance, the abortion clinic opened to provide legal, safe abortions to women with unwanted pregnancies. The initial programs of the four rape crisis organizations were related directly to services to rape victims: court accompaniment, hospital accompaniment, and a rape hotline. These programs grew out of the stated client service goal of providing services to victims of sexual assault or rape.

According to Riger (1984),

> The classic analysis of social movement organizations rooted in the work of Weber (1946) and Michels (1962) asserts that as a movement organization attains a base in society, it is inevitably becomes more bureaucratic and develops more conservative goals as a means of maintaining itself (p. 101).

Goal transformation and goal displacement are two conditions that are well documented in social movement organizations (Simon, 1982; Rothschild and Whitt, 1986). Rothschild and Whitt (1986) describe a variety of circumstances whereby goal displacement occurs:

> (1)   Organizational goals may become increasingly accommodated to contrary values in the surrounding community...(2) organizations...may essentially accomplish their original goals and then shift to more diffuse ones in order to maintain the organization per se...(3) organizations...may find it impossible to realize their original goals and may then develop more diffuse ones...4) procedural regulations and rules (means to attain goals) may become so rigid that they are converted into ends in themselves...and, (5) organization maintenance and growth may be transformed into ends in themselves...(p. 74).

Of the 15 organizations studied, only two displaced their original stated goals for differently stated goals according to current documentation. The original goals of The Crime Victim's Center of Chester County originally incorporated as Rape Crisis Council, changed in 1977 from providing a range of supportive services to victims of sexual assault/abuse (Rape Crisis Council. Charter, July, 1977). The Rape Crisis Council is now one project under the corporate structure of The Crime Victims' Center (M. Gusz, personal communication, September 13, 1989).

Victim Services Center of Montgomery County, originally incorporated as Women Against Rape of Montgomery County, had as its original goal the provision of services to victims of sexual assault or rape (K. Riccio, personal communication, November 6, 1989). This goal changed in 1985 and is currently stated as

To provide supportive services in a nondiscriminatory manner for all individuals who have been victims of serious crime...(Victim Services Center of Montgomery County. <u>Agency History And Services</u>, 1989).

These alterations in original stated goals transformed the organizations' original intentions of serving only victims of sexual assault or rape to serving all victims (male and female) of all violent crimes. In addition to broadening the function of these two organizations, by becoming comprehensive victim services centers, the client population of these organizations deliberately been extended beyond the initial female population whose needs the original goals were designed to meet.

Riger (1984) states, "Organizational goals change because of both internal and external pressures" (p. 107). Both of these organizations displaced original goals when their first major funding source was terminated, and the opportunity to obtain new funding required a goal change, enabling these two organizations to become comprehensive crime victims centers.

Interestingly, neither The Crime Victims' Center of Chester County or Victim Services of Montgomery County are current members of the state-wide coalition of rape crisis centers, Pennsylvania Coalition Against Rape (PCAR), although both organizations subcontract with PCAR to receive state funding to provide specific services to victims of sexual assault or rape. For The Crime Victims' Center of Chester County, the break with PCAR signified a purposeful departure from the feminist philosophy of the state-wide coalition (M. Gusz, personal communication, September 13, 1989). Just a few years earlier, the two founders of Crime Victims' Center had been instrumental in the founding of the state-wide coalition in 1975 by sponsoring the first meeting of all rape crisis centers in Pennsylvania focused on coordination of efforts to help rape victims and to increase public awareness about rape legislation and rape-related issues (M. Gusz, personal communication, September 13, 1989).

Rewriting of initial goal statements occurred in two other organizations, reflecting expansion of original client domains to include either additional female populations and/or different needs of women which the organization was not initially meeting. For example, when the Coordinating Office for Drug and Alcohol Abuse Programs (CODAAP) transferred the leadership of Interim House from internal management to management by an external organization, Philadelphia Health Management Corporation, in 1985, the organization's goals were rewritten to include women's substance abuse. The first grant proposal of 1972 to the Coordinating Office for Drug and Alcohol Abuse Programs (CODAAP) stated the following goals:

(a)   to provide a method of service to rehabilitate women alcoholics; (b) to educate alcoholics and their family in the prevention and arrest of their disease; and, (c) to help the woman to help herself be independent.

However, the current goal statement, found in the organization's 1985 policy and procedures manual, states the following goals:

(a) to facilitate the resident's acceptance of herself as addicted to alcohol and/or other substances and to inculcate the goal of abstinence; (b) to provide a therapeutic milieu in which to conduct an effective residential recovery and rehabilitation program for women who are substance abusers; (c) to help the substance abuser to identify and use alternative methods of dealing with negative emotional responses to stress in place of using a substance...

Another organization, Women In Transition, Inc. (WIT) altered the wording of its original stated goal

to help women realize their potential as strong, independent people, regardless of whether the chose to remain in a marriage, divorce or remarry" (Galper and Washburne, 1976, p. 249)

when, in 1985, the opportunity to obtain funds from the local Coordinating Office for Drug and Alcohol Abuse Programs (CODAAP) to provide outreach, assessment, advocacy and referral of addicted women became available. Acceptance of these funds had the impact of expanding the above statement

to help women realize their fullest potential as strong, capable, independent people with great capacities to succeed in any venture (Women In Transition. Women in Transition Fact Sheet, November 7, 1988).

Although the other 11 organizations retain their original written goal statements, organizational programs have expanded to include female populations different from the original female client populations reflected in their initial goal statements. For example, The Women's Center of Montgomery County has a Korean women's support group; the Women's Resource Center has a single mothers' resource group and a house-sharing program for old and young in Delaware County; and the Philadelphia Women's Network has moved from networking with other business women to providing a mentoring program for newcomers in corporations. Both rape crisis centers, WOAR and Women Against Rape (Delaware County) now serve victims of child sexual abuse and the two domestic violence organizations, A Woman's Place and Domestic Abuse project, now have specialized childrens' programs in their shelters. These programs were not explicitly developed to extend these organizations' goals beyond the female population, however, they have had the effect of doing so.

Those eight organizations that identified social change goals in their initial documentation continue to emphasize such goals. In addition to the already existing educational programs associated with social change goals in a number of new ways. For each new employee, indoctrination to the social change perspective and feminist philosophy of the organization occurs through attendance at required training sessions. Feminist philosophical statements which incorporate the social change goals of the organization have been written and are currently found in policy and procedural manuals of each of these eight organizations. The Women's Center of Montgomery County presents its mission statement, which includes the goal of effecting social change for the betterment of women, on all its printed documentation (D. Byrne, personal communication, September 7, 1989).

Increased preventative efforts in the community are currently emphasized by WOAR and the Domestic Abuse Project. WOAR has drafted plans and is seeking start-up funding for the development of a Training and Research Institute to address sexual assault in a satellite location (Kensington). It is WOAR's intention to target minorities for education on substance abuse, sexual assault, and AIDS, and to provide sensitivity training to neighborhood law officers in this target area in order to decrease the occurrence of sexual assault and rape (K. Kulp, personal communication, August 29, 1989). The Domestic Abuse Project is opening a satellite location in Upper Darby concentrating on prevention, through education and training, of domestic violence in this specific area of Delaware County (M. Bailey, personal communication, August 23, 1989).

To summarize, at their inception, all of the 15 organizations studied stated client service goals in their earliest documentation, while eight of the 15 organizations presented social change goals as well. Two of the 15 organizations deliberately displaced their original goals in order to extend their services and clientele beyond the initial focus and function of serving sexual assault or rape female victims. Two of the organizations rewrote initial goal statements to expand their initial female population to new female populations. Eleven of the organizations have had no written changes in their original goal statements. However, in all 11 of these organizations, the original client service goals and/or social change goals are reflected in current expansion of organizational program activities. In their service delivery survey of 70 women's organizations, Hooyman and Cunningham (1986) found that while

> most of the organizations did not explicitly state a goal of changing current structural conditions, they nevertheless viewed themselves as alternatives to existing systems and therefore as changing the underlying conditions faced by women (p. 174).

In this study, although not written in the original documentation, Women's Suburban Clinic has always had the social change goal of advocacy for the reproductive rights of women (S. Hollos, personal communication, August 2, 1989). A pro-choice stance regarding abortion is currently being reflected by each of the organizations studied. Organizations like Women's Suburban Clinic and WOAR have recently sponsored trips to Harrisburg, Pennsylvania and Washington, D.C. for pro-choice rallies. Organizations such as Women's Center of Montgomery County and Women In Transition have encouraged clients and staff to attend such rallies. In other organizations, individual staff members encourage other staff and clients to attend rallies. Although only eight of the organizations studied have explicit social change goals, the action being taken by organization leaders and individual organization members to promote organized participation in the pro-choice movement suggests that this issue provides a resurgence of the feminist principle of effecting structural change in society for these organizations.

Formalization

Formalization is defined as the extent to which rules, procedures, instructions and communications are written and distributed to everyone (Pugh, et al., 1968, p. 79). Formalization provides an organization with the ability to replicate its work and increase work efficiency. (Weisbord, 1978).

Initial documentation and interviews with founders of the fifteen organizations in this study determined the extent to which they had the following documents at inception: information pamphlet/brochure, personnel manual, procedures manual, job descriptions, organizational chart, and staff meeting minutes. In addition, the development of the above documentation throughout the life cycle of the 15 organizations was traced.

Initially, all of the organizations studied had documents which were used for communication purposes. One external document developed by all 15 organizations was an agency brochure/information pamphlet informing women about its purpose and services. These pamphlets were distributed to other women in the community as a way to gain public attention for the work the organization was doing.

In addition to recruiting clientele, distribution of external communication documents enabled an organization to increase its support, either by finding like-minded women who contributed time and/or money or by getting media coverage. For example, WOAR was able to get sympathetic and viable press coverage by assigning staff (the same two people) to build relationships with the press and by developing cogent and appealing literature packets (Simon, 2983).

The Women's Resource Center developed a flyer to distribute in shopping centers to alert women to the center's existence and encourage them to participate in its programs and become members of the organization (Hopkins, undated). Women In Transition developed a pamphlet containing answers to commonly asked questions about separation and divorce to distribute to women who called their hotline for information . Several years after the organization's inception this pamphlet evolved into a 300 page published manual called *Women in Transition: A Feminist Handbook on Separation and Divorce* and was distributed nationally ("Profile of Lyn McMahon," Universal City News, Friday, March 27, 1987).

Newsletters were the first documents used for internal communication by the organizations studied. They were distributed to all members of an organization, including volunteers, paid members, paid staff and governing board members. Early in their life histories, nine of the 15 organizations in this study began distributing newsletters to all members of the organization and continue to do so to this day. Another organization (Women Against Rape) has recently begun newsletter distribution (J. Dale, personal communication, January 4, 1990). Newsletters gave a more in depth look at the work of an organization, its members and its services. The intent of WOARPATH, Women Organized Against Rape's newsletter, was that it would serve as a forum for ideas and discussion of issues related to rape, as well as a vehicle of information about WOAR (WOAR. WOARPATH, Inaugural Issue, Winter, 1976-77. Available from WOAR, 125 South 9th Street, Suite 601, Philadelphia, PA 19107).

Another document found to exist in all of the organizations was written minutes of their founders' meetings. However, unlike the organizations' newsletters, these minutes were not distributed to anyone except members of the governing body. Whatever the format of the governing body (Board of Directors, Collectives, Steering Committees), minutes recorded the process and decisions made by the founders of the organization on topics such as development or organizational goals and programs as well as defining the organizational structure.

For instance, minutes of board meetings at Interim House began to be recorded in 1971, 2 years before the halfway house opened. At one of the initial board meetings in 1971, the goals of the organization were set down by the founders in writing as part of the minutes. These goals were the basis for the statement of purpose when the organization incorporated in 1971 and constituted the goal statement in the 1982 grant proposal to the Coordinating Office of Drug and Alcohol Abuse Programs.

Written meeting minutes begin the process of formalizing internal communication; they cement a group of individuals together with written rules and procedures developed initially out of individual decisions (Rothschild and Whitt, 1986). In addition, formalization reduced human variability and depersonalizes decision-making (Jackson and Morgan, 1978).

At Domestic Abuse Project in Delaware County, decisions about rules were made as individual situations occurred. The organization had no policies. Members had to sit together and determine what the policy was. These decisions were then recorded in the founders' meeting minutes and were referred to as similar situations repeated themselves. From these meetings, standardized forms and a manual for volunteers were developed (E. Humme, personal communication, September 12, 1989).

The governing body of The Feminist Therapy Collective/The Women's Therapy Center kept minutes of its meetings which helped the constantly changing part-time therapists to make consistent salary decisions. The minutes also facilitated decisions regarding the creation of a board of directors and ending collective decision-making. Organization members communicated issues of concerning in writing for discussion at Collective meetings. These written communications addressed problems of the Collective, such as the focus of the organization's existence largely on satisfaction of the needs of members and the dysfunctional nature of the decision-making process and follow through. These written concerns paved the way for organization members to establish a Task Force and hire an outside consultant. The final Task Force report presented to the Collective concluded that:

> Because the agency recognizes the need for direction and leadership, both short term and long term, it will transform into a more traditional management structure" (The Feminist Therapy Collective, Report of Task Force, 1982).

According to the Weber model of bureaucracy (Jackson and Morgan,

1978), one condition of bureaucracy is the existence of a

well-ordered system of rules and procedures that regulate the conduct of work. Rules serve several purposes: (a) they standardize operations and decision; (b) they serve as receptacles of past learning; (c) they protect incumbents and ensure equality of treatment (p. 73).

According to Powell (1986), who analyzed the political economy of Alternative Service Organizations (ASO),

ASOs often tend to become more formalized as they age. The development of rules, in the form of operating policies and procedures, is a logical result of the organization's experience. From a beginning with no model to follow, the organization creates its own model. Many decisions which once were political become routine and therefore economic (p 66).

At birth, only two of the 15 organizations studied had any type of written manual of rules, procedures or policies. Those two exceptions were organizations connected to women's medical care (Women's Suburban Clinic and The Birth Center) and were required by law to have written medical procedure manuals to perform their services. A written job description for the position of midwife existed at the inception of The Birth Center. For the eight domestic violence and rape centers, the first manual to be written was the volunteer training manual. This was in response to funding requirements of documenting standardized training of volunteers, as required by the respective state coalitions which negotiated with the government for funding. This documentation provided accountability to the coalitions by the organizations for training significant numbers of volunteers.

Powell (1986) identified this occurrence for other alternative organizations as well. He states, "Tighter procedures for accountability may be required by funders..." (p. 67). The three organizations (Women Against Rape, Domestic Abuse Project and Interim House) that received government funding at the beginning of their provision of service were required to submit job descriptions and an organizational chart as part of their proposals. Founders of the Marital Abuse Project put together a fake organizational chart for purposes of the grant application requirements (E. Humme, personal communications, September 12, 1989). Currently, all of the organizations studied have at least one written job description.

Eleven of the 15 organization now have all of the following written documentation: policy and procedure manuals for paid staff, informational brochures/pamphlets, job descriptions and organizational charts.

These documents are available to all organization members. However, written staff meeting minutes are not consistently kept by all 15 of the organizations. In fact, only eight currently record staff meeting minutes. For those organizations that do not keep written staff meeting minutes, staff meetings were described as informal gatherings.

The four organizations that do not have all of the above written documentation have budgets under $100,000, one or no full-time paid staff, and do not receive government funding.

To summarize, for all of the 15 organizations in this study, the degree of formalization has increased. Accountability to outside funding sources has influenced the degree of formalization, with those organizations not receiving outside funding being less formalized. Internally, size of budget and number of paid full-time staff has influenced the extent of formalization, with the smaller organizations less formalized. However, current Boards of Directors for all of the 15 organizations exercise influence on current leaders to formalize organization policies and procedures.

Those organizations that had formalized procedure and policy manuals from the beginning such as Women's Suburban Clinic and The Birth Center, also had greater job specialization at inception than those organizations having no formalized procedure and policy manuals. Greater formalization and job specialization for Women's Suburban Clinic and The Birth Center was associated, initially, with the medical orientation of these organizations. As new, distinct medical services were initiated at both organizations, increased formalization occurred. In addition, Women's Suburban Clinic's counseling department has grown into an important discrete service with its own formalized procedural and policy documentation (S. Hollos, personal communication, August 2, 1989).

In contrast to Women's Suburban Clinic and The Birth Center, other organizations providing non-medical services increased formalization when outside funding, in particular governmental funding, was sought and obtained. One organization Marital Abuse Project, initially formalized documentation only to the extent required by the funding source (E. Humme, personal communication, September 12, 1989). However, as the organization aged, the Board of Directors placed greater emphasis on formalizing procedures. When the organization's founder resigned as Executive Director in 1987, one concern of the Board of Directors was to hire a new director with stronger management skills, specifically in the area of formalizing procedures and policies (M. Bailey, personal communication, August 23, 1989).

In 1977, Interim House leaders were strongly advised by the Coordinating Office for Drug and Alcohol Abuse Programs (CODAAP) to keep better written records of fiscal transactions, organization policies and procedures. Interim House leaders had difficulties meeting CODAAP expectations. In 1985, CODAAP refused to renew Interim House's funding unless the Board of Interim House agreed to CODAAP's contracting with an outside management corporation to manage Interim House. In that year, 1985, the Philadelphia Health Management Corporation's leadership at Interim House developed a procedure and policy manual which was then distributed to all employees (Interim House. Policy and Procedures Manual, 1985).

Those non-medical organizations that depend entirely on membership fees and fees for service (Philadelphia Women's Network, Women for Sobriety and the Women's Therapy Center) have formalized those procedures crucial to the smooth operation of the organization. For example, each part-time therapist at Women's Therapist Center receives a contract explicitly stating policies regarding confidentiality, insurance and fees (J. Biordi, personal communication, August 9, 1989).

The degree of formalization in all 15 of the organizations has increased. Those organizations with a medical purpose were more formalized from inception, while other organizations formalized in response to applying for or obtaining outside funding. Organizations that were subject to no external pressures were slower to formalize. However, with time and maturation, these organizations have increased their formalization efforts as well.

Personal Relationships

Riger (1984) refers to the attraction of women to membership in feminist organizations as based on gaining a feeling of sisterhood and personal acceptance from other women. Personal relationships are of great importance to members of feminist organizations. Similarly, Rothschild and Whitt (1986) found in collectivist-democratic organizations that social relationships are personal and of value in themselves. The organizations in this study evolved out of personal relationships developed from the concerns of founders about specific women's issues. Personal factors had led founders of eight of the organizations to attend consciousness-raising (C-R) groups or women's groups focusing on the issues that concerned them. The two women who founded alcohol programs were recovering alcoholics. One women who founded Marital Abuse Project was going through a divorce; likewise, several of the founders of Women In Transition were involved in divorces.

This concern for the personal in these organizations is in direct contrast to the impersonality which characterizes bureaucracies (Newman, 1980; Davidson, 1980, Rothschild and Whitt, 1986). Impersonality is the extent to which both organizational members and outsiders are treated without regard to individual qualities (Hall, 1963).

Another feature characterizing alternative organizations, such as collectives and feminist organizations, as different from bureaucracies is the homogeneity of the members (Rothschild and Whitt, 1986). The organizations in this study attracted people with similar political views and experiences, who identified with social movements. Although the founder of Women Organized Against Rape had not experienced rape herself, she knew someone who had. Her friend's experience prompted her to begin her crusade (J. Pinto, personal communication, November 18, 1989). Similarly, concern for others who had been raped prompted the founders of Crime Victim's Center in Chester County to organize (M. Gusz, personal communication, September 13, 1989). The founders of Women Against Rape were involved in the Women's Action Coalition on a committee concerning sexual assault and wanted to put into action their beliefs about improving the treatment of rape victims (J. Dale, personal communication, January 4, 1990).

Personal connection to other women was the key to the beginnings of these organizations. As Rothschild and Whitt beginnings of these organizations. As Rothschild and Whitt (1986) point out, "Relationships are to be wholistic, affective, and of value in themselves" (p. 55). This finding was true for the workers collectives studied by Newman (1980) and the alternative organizations studied by Davidson (1980).

At birth and early in the organizations' life cycle, the hiring of new staff and/or volunteers was based on their moral/value commitment rather than on educational and/or experiential credentials. For those organizations that relied on outside funding, some attention to funding expectations in relation to credentials had to be adhered to. For instance, at Interim House, which relied exclusively on CODAAP funding, friends of the founder, whom she had known at another alcohol program, were hired to satisfy funding requirements (G. Walters, personal communication, August 17, 1989). Although the therapists at the Feminist Therapy Collective had educational requirements for the hiring of new therapists, those who were hired were also screened with regard to their commitment to the concept of feminist therapy (P. Mikols, personal communication, September 6, 1989). An original volunteer at WOAR stated that she affiliated with the organization first as a volunteer and than as administrator because she like the women of WOAR (B. Simon, personal communication, November 18, 1989). This is a common theme heard from original volunteers and paid staff in all the organizations.

Also common to the organizations that originally were all-volunteer was the tendency of volunteers to become paid staff. As the organizations evolved, at six of the seven organizations begun as all-volunteer organizations, one or more of their volunteers became paid staff members.

Subsequently, according to Newman (1980), in the worker collectives she studied, and also documented by four of the six organizations in this study, a division of labor, power and status was created between paid and volunteer staff, shifting what was once important to all, the personal, to a concern for the task by the paid staff. In her 1980 study, Newman identifies an "old" versus "new" distinction:

> Salaried staff were recruited from the original membership of the collectives. New participants had to enter on an entirely different basis. Thus the 'salaried' versus 'volunteer' dichotomy paralleled an 'old' versus 'new' distinction (p. 155).

Similar issues were identified by members of the organizations in this study. At the Women's Center of Montgomery County, there is concern that volunteers have lost ownership of the organization to paid staff. In addition, an oldtimer complains that the new volunteers do not have the same commitment as the oldtimers (B. Sayre, personal communication, November 10, 1989). At the Domestic Abuse Project, questions of who is more important, volunteers or paid staff, are raised continuously, and at the Women's Resource Center, a power struggle between volunteer and paid staff for control of the organization's daily operation is underway. In addition, other areas of conflict have arisen within the 15 organizations studied that have moved the concern from the personal to a concern with "getting the job done."

One area in which the personal has moved to a concern with professional accomplishment is in the hiring procedure for professionals. Hiring procedures for all professionals in the organizations studied are now based on job descriptions which have experiential and/or education requirements. They now require more than a value system/moral commitment to a cause. In addition, all but two of the organizations studied now have at least one full-time paid employee and all have at least one part-time employee. Two of the four organizations with budgets of $100,000 or less are organizations with no full-time paid staff, but both have at least one part-time paid staff.

However, despite the increased impersonality in hiring and in concern for getting the task done, the members' interest in and commitment to the cause for which the organization stands and to which it is dedicated still exists in the organizations studied. Concurrent membership in other feminist social, political and service organizations, such as the National Abortion Rights Action League, the National Association of Women, and women's commissions on issues such as drugs and alcohol, occurs in all of the organizations. In addition, founding members of 11 of the organizations still maintain some current connection to those organizations. Of the four organizations with no founding member currently affiliated, two had, until 2 years ago, an original founder as executive director. Five of the organizations still have their original founder as executive director. Five of the organizations still have their original executive director or a founder as the current executive director.

Three of the organizations have advertised the executive directors' position in national feminist literature, and have included in the advertisement the requirement of a feminist/pro-choice perspective. And, specifically, for one organization (Women's Resource Center), a pro-choice perspective for employment is an unwritten expectation of the Board of Directors (S. Staas, personal communication, December 4, 1989).

Four of the organizations have promoted their current executive from within the organization, while six of the organizations have hired individuals outside the organization for the position of executive director.

Regardless of the source of recruitment of the current executive, Boards of Directors chose women with strong personal connections to feminism. For instance, the new executive of A Women's Place is formerly the executive of a rape center in California; the new executive of Women In Transition has worked within the Philadelphia' women's movement since the 1970's; and the new executive of the Domestic Abuse Project has a strong feminist base.

To conclude, the 15 organizations studied have become more impersonal in their concerns for getting the task done, as evidenced by more stringent educational/experiential requirements for staff positions, as well as by the movement of focus of control from volunteers to paid staff. However, in most of the organizations, one or more of the original founders are still connected to the organization and most new organization members are committed to the original purpose of the organization. Feminist philosophy statements exist in some form in 13 of the 15 organizations studied This connection to feminist ideology keeps the personal alive in these organizations.

Rewards

A reward system motivates performance (Katz and Kahn, 1966) and participation in the organization (Rothschild and Whitt, 1986) by providing different types of incentives to the individual member. These incentives can be purposive (value fulfillment), friendship, and/or material (pay) incentives (Zald & Ash Garner, 1987). According to Rosthchild & Whitt (1988), "Alternative organizations often appeal to symbolic values to motivate people to join and to participate" (p. 57).

For example, joining a rape or domestic violence organization represented to a member the fight for freedom for herself and other women from the oppression of male dominance (E. Humme, personal communication, September 12, 1989).

At inception and into their early phases of organizational development, the reward systems of the organizations studied emphasized purposive and solidary rewards. Seven of the organizations started with all volunteers and no paid staff, one of the organizations had equal pay for all employees, and, in one of the organizations, members were paid equally when there was money and, when there was not, they went on unemployment in order to support themselves while writing grants to obtain new funding. For all of the 15 organizations, founders' personal beliefs, value and interests led to their involvement with the particular issue of the organization which they founded. The founder of the Marital Abuse Project reports that she was undergoing a divorce at the time she became connected with the Women's Action Coalition and was looking for support from other women going through the same process. According to this woman, the experience of founding the Marital Abuse Project of the Women's Action Coalition enhanced her self-image and give her a feeling of empowerment (E. Humme, personal communication, September 12, 1989). Similarly, the founder of The Feminist Therapy Collective reported that her enhanced self-image was a benefit of actualizing a dream she had about starting a feminist therapy center (S. Elias, personal communication, September 19, 1989).

A reward reaped by the founding therapists of The Feminist Therapy Center was establishment of their own therapy practice. The original founding therapists got paid equally, regardless of experience, in a minimum amount ($2.00 per hour). In fact, the founding therapists of The Feminist Therapy Center began the Center by contributing their own money as well as time (S. Elias, personal communication, September 19, 1989).

This phenomenon is not unique to The Feminist Therapy Center. The founders of two other organizations, A Woman's Place and Women for

Sobriety, agreed to commit their own money and time to their organizations' development for more than 1 year. However, after the first year of operation, when A Woman's Place decided to hire a shelter director, although each of the founders was interested in the position, the salary was too low for any of them to leave their other jobs (B. Frantz, personal communication, 1989). The founder of Marital Abuse Project stated that, if it were not for the personal rewards she experienced, she would never have accepted such a low salary (E. Humme, personal communication, September 12, 1989).

The fact that inadequate salaries exist in alternative organizations is substantiated in this study as well as in Rothschild and Whitt's (1986) study of collective workplaces. The state, "Alternative institutions generally provide woefully inadequate levels of remuneration by the standards of our society" (p. 57). In the organizations studied here, funds for salaries would often have to be cut into small chunks so that everyone could receive something. This was also found to be true in Newman's 1980 study of worker collectives.

For example, when, in the early life of two organizations, it was difficult to make ends meet, top management worked without compensation. This occurred at the Women's Suburban Clinic, where the executive/founder and medical director took pay cuts, due to early financial problems. Early in the organization's life of the Women's Suburban Clinic, the executive who had authority to make salary increases did so to all but herself, the head nurse, and the medical director. During the first year of The Birth Centers existence, the method of payment changed from salary to per diem. This resulted in a high turnover of midwives during this change (S. Hollos, personal communication, August 2, 1989).

In addition, at inception, 12 of the organizations had more part-time than full-time employees, enabling these organizations to divide their funds among as many paid staff members as possible. This circumstance was found in the collectives studied by Newman (1980) as well. In one of the organizations in this study, Women's Center of Montgomery County, the executive director position has been shared, the salary halved and, in two of the organizations, Philadelphia Women's Network and Women's Therapy Center, the only paid positions are part-time. These two organizations have no executive directors and have budgets of under $100,000.

Rothschild and Whitt (1986) point out,

> In these organizations, as much as in any, there exists an important coalescence of material and ideal interests. Even volunteers in these organizations, whose motives on the face of it would appear to be wholly idealistic,

also have material incentives (p. 57).

This was substantiated in the 15 organizations studied in a number of ways. First, for the seven organizations that began as all-volunteer organizations, one or more of the original volunteers moved into a paid position. All 13 organizations that have volunteers in their organizations have also seen volunteer staff move into paid staff positions. In fact, similar priority is given to volunteers, when job positions become open, as is given to current staff for promotion.

Second, eight of the organizations have always had pay differentials among paid staff, dependent upon job position, part-time/full-time status, and experience and education. Decisions regarding pay differentials were made not by the employees, but by governing bodies such as steering committees, board of directors, or by executive directors.

One of the organizations, Women Against Rape, is unique in its method of giving increments. Increments of the same amount are given regardless of job position to all employees (J. Dale, personal communication, January 4, 1990). Two organizations, Women's Suburban Clinic and The Birth Center, have unusual sick leave policies which are extended to the health care of family members and are based on employees need (S. Hollos, personal communication, August 2, 1989).

The practice of employing part-time staff currently exists in all of the organizations studied. One of the organizations, A Women's Place, provides full-time benefits to all part-time staff. This organization rewards its part-time employees in this manner because of its need to retain a large number of part-time workers to supervise the women living in the Shelter on a 24-hour basis (B. Webber, personal communication, October 26, 1989). The seven organizations that evolved from a volunteer staff base to a current emphasis on paid staff now stress material rewards for paid staff, part-time and full-time. One of the problems which occurred in this changeover from a volunteer to a paid staff model is conflict between volunteer and paid staff for control of decision-making as well as provision of direct services. This is currently an issue for the members of the Women's Resource Center (S. Stass, personal communication, December 4, 1989). This conflict creates a divisiveness between organization members and places limitations on friendships being formed, according to the organization's member's status as either a volunteer or a paid staff member (V. Gutter, personal communication, October 5, 1989).

Currently, paid staff members of all 15 organizations are concerned about material rewards. The executives of the organizations with formal professional counseling components, such as WOAR, Women's Therapy

Center, Domestic Abuse Project and Women's Suburban Clinic, recognize the importance of competitive salaries in order to maintain quality staff. Currently, eight of the organizations' executives feel that salaries are competitive with similar organizations, while executives of four other organizations feel salaries are not competitive. Two executives feel salaries are moderately competitive. For three organizations, this question was not answered.

Competitive salary is one type of reward existing in these organizations; but today, as well as at the time of the founding of these organizations, purposive rewards are of importance to organization members in all of the organizations studied. The Executive Director of Women Against Rape pointed out that, since its founding in 1976, there has been little turnover of staff, which she attributes to the staff's commitment to the goal of the organization which is to eliminate rape in our society (J. Dale, personal communication, January 4, 1990). This founder has been Executive Director of the organization since its inception. For more than half of the 15 organizations studied, one or more individuals connected with the organization at inception retained a current connection to the organization either as an executive director, board member or consultant. Five of the current executive directors were original executive directors and founders of their organizations. When questioned as to why these individuals have remained with the organization for 10 years or more, the response of "a continuing commitment to the cause" was uniform.

The importance of establishing friendships now exists primarily within the volunteer base of these organizations. Philadelphia Women's Network's volunteer membership meets once a month to network and develop friendships based on similar career interests and issues (N. Pigford, personal communication, July 18, 1989). The volunteers at Women's Resource Center socialize together, frequently meeting away from the Center (V. Gutter, personal communication, October 5, 1989). The Executive Director at Crime Victims' Center of Chester County has experienced difficulty obtaining volunteers due to what she describes as the change in volunteers' ability to socialize with one another. Currently, volunteers at Crime Victims' Center of Chester County are utilized to supplement the role of professional staff during off hours and have less of an opportunity to socialize with each other (M. Gusz, personal communication, September 12, 1989). On the other hand, three executive directors interviewed discourage socializing among staff, feeling that such socializing interferes with getting the job done.

For the first time in the organization's history, supervisory staff of A Women's Place has been moved out of the Shelter and into a separate building. The purpose of this move, according to the Executive Director, was to increase these individuals' efficiency in their roles as managers. The Executive Director reports resistance on the part of oldtimers to comply with this separation, due to their reluctance to give up the camaraderie developed within the Shelter (B. Webber, personal communication, October 26, 1989).

To conclude, the 15 organizations studied have developed a multi-faceted reward system over time reflecting a more diverse reward system than found at these organizations' inception. Today, a major difference from the reward system of 10 or more years ago is to change from volunteer to paid staff. With this change, material rewards were introduced into the already existing purposive and friendship reward systems of those organizations that were initially all-volunteer.

Material rewards are important, but so are purposive rewards. Both have bearing on the hiring and retention of paid staff. It is felt by all of the current leaders interviewed that commitment to the purpose of the organization influences paid staff members' decisions to seek and maintain employment at these organizations.

Other personal rewards are also found to result from affiliation with these organizations. For instance, the Women's Therapy Center provides a solid stepping stone for psychotherapists to move on to private practice (J. Biordi, personal communication, August 9, 1989). One former Executive Director ran for political office using her relationship with County officials to her political advantage (B. Frantz, personal communication, November 20, 1989). The founder and current Executive Director of Women for Sobriety has been able to promote publications of her three books through this organization (J. Kirkpatrick, personal communication, July 31, 1989).

Although the development of friendships may still be a motivating factor for volunteers joining these 15 organizations, their ability to socialize is more limited than during the inception of volunteers, who now supplement the work activity of paid staff, and disencouragement by executives of socializing among volunteers or paid staff during the work day.

Division of Labor

Division of labor is defined as the extent to which work tasks are subdivided by functional specialization in the organization (Hall, 1963). Work can be divided by function and by product or a mixture of both (Weisbord, 1976). According to Rothschild and Whitt (1986), in alternative organizations, there is a generalization of jobs and functions, with minimal division of labor. It is the

> aim to eliminate the bureaucratic division of labor that separates intellectual worker from manual worker, administrative tasks from performance tasks (p. 59).

In this study, initially, eight of the 15 organizations did not have any formalized differentiation of labor among organization members. For six of these organizations, a combination of volunteers and paid staff all did the same jobs. For two others, The Feminist Therapy Collective and Women In Transition (WIT), at start-up, there were no volunteers, as it was felt that the volunteer concept was not feminist, so all staff members were paid and did all jobs.

WIT documents the difficulties of running an organization with no job differentiation.

> There was no time that we were not on call, either to write a proposal overnight or deal with an emergency situation. We never left the job at the office... (Galper & Washburne, 1976, p. 51).

Their first division of labor was to move to a coordinating team of three which was delegated the day-to-day administrative tasks. This evolved into a co-director model and eventually to one executive director (S. L. McMahon, personal communication, August 3, 1989).

At its birth, the Marital Abuse Project used different job titles, due to funding proposal requirements; but, in reality, staff met each week to distribute the work according to skill, interest, resources and time. From its founding, the Marital Abuse Project, which changed its name in 1980 to the Domestic Abuse Project, had co-directors until one of the co-directors left the agency. At that time, the Board of Directors, whose membership had been opened to the community, decided not to support the co-director model and instituted the executive director model. Specialized functional job titles, such as program coordinator, resource coordinator, Media office coordinator, and hotline coordinator were also established at that time (E. Humme, personal communication, September 12, 1989).

Founding members of the Feminist Therapy Collective were all therapists and were described by one of the founders as an undifferentiated mass of solidarity (P. Mikols, personal communication, September 6, 1989). However, the first job specified was coordinator, whose responsibility it was to take over the jobs necessary to the maintenance of the collective, such as scheduling appointments and billing clients, which the therapists formerly shared.

For those organizations that were all-volunteer and had no division of labor but instead shared job responsibilities, the first job position filled was an administrative one, either as the president of a board of directors, executive director or as an administrative coordinator.

As Rothschild and Whitt (1986) point out:

> collectivist forms of organization are undermined to the extent that the knowledge and skills needed to perform the organization's tasks (be they medical knowledge, legal know-how, or whatever) are unevenly distributed (p. 104).

In the case of the two medical organizations, The Birth Center and Women's Suburban Clinic, the need for technical knowledge in the form of medical training and expertise limited the ability of organization members to share jobs and necessitated specialization from the start. The Women's Suburban Clinic initially used volunteers from Planned Parenthood and the Junior League in the receptionist role, but due to the sensitive nature of the services (abortion), volunteers were replaced by trained staff. The role of the volunteer was eventually eliminated from this organization (S. Hollos, personal communication, August 2, 1989).

At inception, the two rape crisis centers studied divided their work according to specialization. For example, WOAR divided its work into committees which focused on different aspects of the problem of rape, specifically legal, medical, community education, and volunteer development. The founder of WOAR deliberately chose women who were experts in these areas so that the foundation of the organization would be strong for future program development (J. Pinto, personal communication, November 18, 1989).

The Women's Center of Montgomery County divided its work into committees pertaining to domestic violence, consciousness-raising, employment, and medical issues. Interestingly, in this organization's early life, one of the committees (domestic violence) became more powerful than the others, resulting in the formation of a new organization (a domestic violence shelter) and the loss of members, money and, temporarily, a focus for the Women's Center (B. Sayre, personal communication, November 10, 1989).

Both Women Organized Against Rape and the Women's Center of Montgomery County identified another problem with the committee structure: confusion concerning authority, responsibilities, and direction for action.

Questions like "Does the Board direct each volunteer? Does the Board direct Staff? What should the organization chart look like" were asked by Board, volunteers and paid staff committee members (D. Byrne, personal communication, September 7, 1989). At WOAR, committees evolved into teams with more specific job positions associated with each discrete team area (medical, legal and education) for action. In this way, clearer job responsibilities developed within each team (K. Kulp, personal communication, August 29, 1989). These two organizations experienced the committee structure difficulties cited in the organizational literature by Jackson and Morgan (1978). They state:

> Committees have been criticized for wasting time, encouraging compromise, and violating the chain of command among other things (p. 149).

Newman (1980), Davidson (1980), Epstein, Russell, and Silvern (1988), as well as this study, found that, over time, alternative organizations such as collectives and feminist organizations become more specialized in their division of labor. This finding supports the systems theory of specialization (Katz and Kahn, 1978) that, over time, more specialization is considered a healthy, even necessary, organizational response to increased need for coordination of function among workers.

Specialization is most often measured by the number of discrete job titles in an organization (Katz & Kahn, 1978). In this study, the number of discrete job titles was counted at year one and at the current year. The results of this count are listed in Table 5.1.

In addition, the 15 organizations studied here became more specialized in two major areas: management and clinical services. For seven of these organizations, financial management has become a specialized position where four of the 15 organizations break fiscal management into two discrete job positions: financial management and fund development.

Epstein, Russell and Silvern's 1988 survey results from 111 shelters indicate that:

> Together the results suggest that shelters did not just get 'bigger' and 'richer' as they developed, but instead grew in particular ways, that is, with specialized roles (p. 361).

In her study of 12 collectives, Newman (1980) found that

> full time staff was rapidly becoming more specialized in certain phases of organizational management (p. 155).

Data Analysis

Number of Discrete Job Titles
(includes paid full-time and part-time)

Name of Organization	Year One	Current Year (1989)	Areas of Job Title Expansion
WSC	7	+15	clinical counselors
WOAR	8	+20	management & counseling
DAP	1	+20	management & programs
WIT	1	11	financial & fund management
TBC	4	12	specialized nursing positions; no counselor positions
Interim House	5	12	financial management
CVC	0	9	financial; project director
WAR	2	10	project director
VCS	0	10	project director; data entry operator
WCMC	0	8	paid staff managers of each office
AWP	0	6	program coordinator
TWC	1	3	administrative coordinator; clinical coordinator
WFS	1	3	
WRC	0	4	all currently part-time
PWN	0	1	administrative assistant

Table 5.1

In this study, the two organizations with the largest budgets and the highest numbers of paid staff are Women Organized Against Rape and Women's Suburban Clinic. WOAR began completely with volunteers who divided their work according to program committees headed by co-chairwomen. Currently, WOAR has more than 20 different job titles, including five director positions (executive director, associate director, developmental director, fiscal director, and clinical director). These mangers make up a management team who are instrumental in day-to-day decision-making. The clinical component of the organization is now composed entirely of professional, degree individuals with specialized training in issues specifically affecting rape victims, such as health care, emergency medical care, and legal care (K. Kulp, personal communication, August 29, 1989).

Women's Suburban Clinic began with seven job titles and currently has more than 15. The major change in this organization's job positions is the addition of a psychotherapeutic component to the already existing (at inception) medical component. The psychotherapy component brought additional non-medical professionals to this organization in the roles of clinical coordinator and contextual counselors. The therapists all have graduate degrees, post-graduate training, and maintain active membership in the Center of Contextual Therapy and Allied Studies (Women's Suburban Clinic. Counseling Services Brochure, undated).

The organization exhibiting the greatest increase in specialization is the Domestic Abuse Project. There are several reasons for its tremendous specialized growth. First, the Domestic Abuse Project has two specialized branches in addition to its headquarters. One branch is a shelter for battered women emphasizing parenting skills as well as children's programs and the other branch is located in a Courthouse, emphasizing legal issues. In addition, the Domestic Abuse Project recently added an additional layer of job positions and created a management team. The specific job responsibilities of each management team member concern decision-making in an assigned program or financial area (M. Bailey, personal communication, August 23, 1989).

Even the four organizations with budgets of $100,000 or less and only part-time paid staff have become more specialized since their inception. Each of these four organizations now has a job title for every role. For instance, the Women's Resource Center began with no job titles or positions. Currently, however, it has four discrete job titles of Director, Housing Coordinator, Single Parent Coordinator and Volunteer Coordinator (S. Staas, personal communication, December 4, 1989). Women for Sobriety has three employees all with different job titles. Although each position has its own specific job responsibilities, there is still much sharing of work among the staff (J. Kirkpatrick, personal communication, July 31, 1989). The Feminist Therapy Collective has grown from one job position of therapist to a clinical coordinator and an administrative coordinator, both of whom are therapists as well (J. Biordi, personal communication, August 9, 1989).

In addition to division of labor becoming more specialized, the organizations studied have become more professional, particularly in the clinical area, where volunteers have been replaced by paid professional staff. At inception, volunteers performed counseling tasks which are now performed by trained professional counselors. At WOAR, the one area to which volunteers are not assigned is the counseling program (K. Kulp, personal communication, August 29, 1989). At the other rape crisis center and at the two comprehensive victims centers, volunteers are now used to perform work that is supplemental to the work of the professional staff. According to the current executives, professionalization adds credibility to the organization with funding sources. As the first feminist organization to affiliate with United Way, WIT had to increase its professionalism at United Way's request (S. L. McMahon, personal communication, August 3, 1989). In addition, current organization leaders express the belief that professionalism maximizes service delivery to clients.

In conclusion, the organizations in this study replicate the findings of other studies of alternative organizations (Newman, 1980; Davidson, 1980; Epstein, Russell, Silvern, 1988) which have, over time, become more specialized as evidenced by the increased number of job titles. As pointed out by Katz and Kahn (1978), job specialization increases coordination and maximizes efficiency in accomplishing job tasks. Current leaders of these 15 organizations are concerned with task accomplishment which, regardless of type of funding source, enhances opportunities for additional funding. Several of these organizations are further specializing in the area of fund development and financial management by placing emphasis on statistical data management. Statistical information is required by funding sources and identifies increased need for funding as well as for new program development. In addition, there is an increased emphasis on community education and training as evidenced by the recent creation of job positions as Director of this topical area at both WOAR and at the Domestic Abuse Project. New funding is now available for efforts in this area by these two organizations.

However, Epstein, Russell, and Silvern (1988) point out that

the movement from reliance on voluntary to increasingly differentiated paid labor represents a major organizational shift that creates the possibility for conflict, as well as the opportunity for ongoing discussion and involvement by workers and residents in the shift (p. 364).

For the organizations in this study that have shifted from volunteer to paid labor with increased job specialization and the elimination of volunteers in performing the more professional, specialized roles, there has been conflict between these two groups, as well as an openness to discuss, confront and experiment with different communication formats. This is best illustrated by the experience of the Domestic Abuse Project, in which volunteers played a major role at the beginning of the organization's life, but are currently feeling devalued, isolated and omitted from the internal power structure. This coincides with the resignation of the founder as Executive Director and hiring of an executive director from outside the organization (M. Bailey, personal communication, August 23, 1989).

In order to address this conflict, Board-appointed committees, encompassing Board members, staff members and volunteers, provide an avenue for discussion. In addition, the Domestic Abuse Project hired an outside consultant to bring in fresh ideas on how to structure the organization so that its feminist principle of empowerment does not get lost in the shift to task specialization. In addition, at frequent retreats, organizational members examine methods of improving communication among the different job positions (M. Bailey, personal communication, August 23, 1989).

Authority Structure

According to Rothschild and Whitt (1986), it is

the basis of authority that distinguishes the collectivist organization from any variant of bureaucracy. The collectivist-democratic organization rejects bureaucratic justifications for authority. Here authority rests not with the individual, whether on the basis of incumbency in office or expertise, but resides in the collectivity (p. 51).

The collective structure allows for compliance to the consensus of the collective which is always fluid and open to negotiation (Rothschild and Whitt, 1986). In opposition to the collective structure, in a hierarchical structure, authority resides in individuals by virtue of incumbency in office and/or expertise. The locus of decision-making is prestructured by the organization (Hall, 1963).

In this study, eight of the 15 organizations began with collective structures, with all members having equal power in the decision-making process and with required consensus in decision-making (Rothschild and Whitt, 1986). For these eight organizations, founders documented the relationship between the organization's collective structure and their feminist belief in empowerment in their early writings, such as Board minutes, feminist philosophy statements, and mission statements.

For instance, at inception, members of the Women In Transition planning group relied on their political ideological perspective rather than any formalized process for decision-making. This "planning group" was responsible for major policy decisions while working collectively running the program (S. L. McMahon, personal communication, August 3, 1989). In its first newsletter, founders of the Women's Center of Montgomery County wrote the following descriptive statement about the organization's structure:

> The structure of the organization will be set up in the form of a coalition or collective similar to New England town meetings where the policy making is divided among us and each of us is an equal sponsor of the project. Every women actively participating in the work of the Center will be a member of the coalition with one vote (Women's Center of Eastern Montgomery, Womenews, November, 1975).

A member of The Feminist Therapy Collective described the relationship between the collective structure and feminism as:

> each decision is made collectively and based on principles of feminism and collective operation working together on an equal, non-hierarchical basis with a quorum necessary on decisions from reupholstering the couch to hiring of a new therapist (P. Mikols, personal communication, September 6, 1989).

Founders of the other six organizations made conscious decisions to structure their organizations in a more traditional manner for a variety of reasons, such as funding requirements, retaining of control by the founder, and greater efficiency in getting the job done with a hierarchical structure. Although these organizations were hierarchical, with at least one person such as the executive director deemed higher in authority than the others, the hierarchies of these organizations were actually relatively flat, with only one layer below the top.

For instance, at start-up, all of the job positions at The Birth Center, such as Director of Midwifery, Medical Director, Director of Newborn

Care were on an equal level. However, conflict regarding whose authority was more important occurred between the Director of Midwifery and
the Medical Director. When the Director of Midwifery left the organization during the early phase of the organization, the structure was changed
by the Board and the Executive Director to a more hierarchical configu-
ration with increased layers of authority (S. Hollos, personal communication, August 2, 1989).

Riger (1984) states,

> The feminist ideology which gives rise to the creation of many Feminist
> Movement Organizations is likely to result in a collectivist organizational
> structure. Yet that type of structure will, in turn, present certain organiza-
> tional dilemmas for Feminist Movement Organizations: slowness of deci-
> sion-making procedures, emotional intensity of interactions, inequitable
> influence processes within groups that value equality, difficulty holding
> members accountable, and the demands of growth (p. 105).

One or more of the dilemmas identified above were found to exist in
all eight of the organizations structured as collectives at birth. Ultimately,
all eight changed from collective to hierarchical structures with centralized decision-making.

Six years after its founding, a member of one organization, who had
been with the collective since its beginning, wrote a letter to a Task Force
charged with investigation of the financial difficulties of the collective.
One of the problems within the organization discussed in her letter was
the dysfunctional nature of the collective decision-making process and
follow through (D. Chambless, Letter to the Task Force, 1980).

A founder of Women in Transition has stated that, as that collective
grew to seven members and included women of different socio-economic,
education and racial backgrounds, it became vulnerable to power plays,
with no process provided for delegation of tasks, accountability, or decision-making.

> At times whether staff should wear bras to work or shave underarms to go
> on TV programs took up equal time with questions about applying for
> federal research funds (McMahon, Undated).

In this organization, as well as at the Women's Resource Center, when
original collective members left to do other things with their lives (such
as to return back to school), the collective structure was replaced by a
different structure in which policy-making was separated from day-to-
day operations. For all of the organizations, initiation of a hierarchical

structure took place through the establishment of one or more director positions or establishment of a formal Board of Directors or both.

When the Victim Services Center of Montgomery County and the Crime Victims' Center of Chester County changed their names, signifying broader representation of all victims of crimes, their authority structures also changed to hierarchical forms, along with the creation of Boards of Directors.

Ultimately, all nine organizations that began with collective structures moved to hierarchical structures with centralized decision-making. This finding is consistent with the findings of other researchers (Newman, 1980; Davidson, 1980; Hooyman and Cunningham, 1986; Epstein, Russell and Silvern, 1988). It should be noted, however, that each of these studies documented the move to hierarchical structures to different degrees.

Newman (1980) concluded that the collectives in her ethnohistorical study were no longer egalitarian in their decision-making process, with one set of staff (paid) having more power over the other (volunteers), although decision-making in group meetings still occurred. In a participant-observation study of eight alternatives, Davidson (1980) found that

> this sample of eight organizations was successful in containing the growth of bureaucratic structures resisting these structural features when they reached a subjective point – a point where the organization began to look and feel like a traditional organization (p. 300).

Hooyman and Cunningham (1986) found that more than half of the women's organizations in their survey described themselves as hierarchical. However, their study reports the majority of the women's organizations used relatively informal consensual approaches to conflict resolution and in policy-making. Epstein, Russell, and Silvern (1988) found that for the 111 shelters responding to their questionnaire, that

> regardless of age, most of the respondents reported a reliance on executive directors or boards of directors for decisions about staff salaries, and few shelters operating on the basis of consensus for such important decisions (p. 361).

All of the organizations in this study were found to rely on executives and boards for policy decisions, such as pay increments, fringe benefits changes, and filing grievance procedures. At the Domestic Abuse Project, a recent decision about reducing sick time by the Board left the staff feeling disempowered (M. Bailey, personal communication, August 23, 1989). At A Women's Place, the Board has recently developed a written grievance procedure as a result of an unsatisfactory experience in the hiring of a previous Executive Director (B. Frantz, personal communication, November 20, 1989).

The larger organizations in this study, WOAR, Domestic Abuse Project and Women's Suburban Clinic, have increased their layers of hierarchy by separating management functions from direct service functions with a middle management layer. Decisions about running the organization are made by management and a chain of command with four hierarchical layers has been established.

At the Domestic Abuse Project, the new Executive Director instituted a "director" layer, which increases accountability in decision-making and better identifies the locus of responsibility for decisions (M. Bailey, personal communication, August 23, 1989). WOAR and Domestic Abuse Project both have a management team composed of the directors. These teams are responsible for policy decisions affecting daily operations of the organization.

In all of the organizations, however, staff participate in decisions on hiring new staff, as it concerns their direct functions. Ultimate authority resides with the executive or board. Ideas for new programs are generated from the direct service staff and are taken up the hierarchical ladder for approval.

To conclude, all the organizations in this study have moved in the direction of a bureaucratic structure with a "hierarchy of positions such that every position is controlled by a higher one" (Jackson and Morgan, 1982, p. 73). Both WOAR and Domestic Abuse Project have recently instituted a hierarchical layer of "director." This layer lies between the executive director position and the coordinator position. Individuals performing jobs as directors do not perform direct service functions, whereas the layer below the "director" level or coordinator mixes together administrative and direct service work as part of their job responsibilities. The creation of this additional hierarchical layer transforms WOAR's structure from a "flat hierarchical structure" to a traditional hierarchical structure (K. Kulp, personal communication, August 29, 198). According to WOAR's current Executive Director, the flat hierarchical structure, in which the distance from line staff to the top was very short, caused considerable confusion for individuals performing too many different functions, both administrative and direct service. Although the distance from line staff has increased, WOAR's current Executive Director feels decisions are now in fact made more quickly and tasks are performed more effectively and efficiently. In addition, WOAR's Executive Director has been able to increase her own decision-making power separate from the Board of Directors, which speeds decisions as well (K. Kulp, personal communication, August 29, 1989). This progression, as illustrated by WOAR, from a collective structure to a flat hierarchical structure, and, eventually, to a traditional hierarchical structure, has occurred at the Domestic Abuse Project as well. The other organizations studied are at varying degrees of this process, depending upon their organizational size. All of the organizations with more than three employees have an administrative position on a distinct hierarchical level, separating the Executive Director from rank-and-file staff. In some organizations, however, this position, Project Director, performs a combination of administrative and direct service tasks.

The Women's Therapy Center's organizational structure was identified by the administrative coordinator as circular rather than hierarchical, with the Board of Directors, the two coordinators, and the other part-time therapists constituting this circular relationship. However, in reality, the decision-making process travels up a chain of command, with the two coordinators as conduits of information between the Board and the other therapists (J. Biordi, personal communication, August 9, 1989).

Additional Findings

This descriptive analysis of the six dimensions for the 15 organizations studied provides an understanding of the change, over time, from these organization's alternative forms to more traditional bureaucratic forms. This finding is consistent with the findings of other research studying change, over time, of alternative organizations (Newman, 1980; Davidson, 1980; Simon, 1982; Riger, 1984; Epstein, Russell and Silvern, 1988).

However, 13 of the 15 feminist organizations studied continue to distinguish themselves as different from traditional organizations, although no longer alternative in form. These 13 organizations have retained their original feminist client service goals which have directed organizational activity throughout their life cycles. Program expansion has been specifically developed to meet the needs of female client populations. Those eight organizations that identified social change goals in their initial documentation continue to emphasize those goals in their community education and outreach programs, staff indoctrination, and frequent in-service training.

In addition, dimensions such as continuing active commitment to the cause for which the organization was founded, valuing of process by organization members, and the characteristics of current organization leaders are other differences distinguishing today's feminist organizations from traditional organizations.

Commitment To Feminist Principles

A strong sense of commitment to the feminist principles on which the founding of these organizations was based 10 or more years ago is still expressed by many of the organizations studied. Feminist philosophy statements exist in current documentation such as newsletters, pamphlets, and brochures. The brochure of A Woman's Place include the following philosophy statement:

> We believe that violence against women has its roots in, and is perpetuated by a society that gives men permission to maintain control over women…Battering is precipitated by the unequal status of women, the lack of viable alternatives, the privatization of the family, an ineffective judiciary and a lack of community sanctions against it (A Woman's Place, Brochure, undated).

One of the organizations studied formalized its feminist philosophy into a written statement in 1987 and another of the organizations studied developed a motto encouraging empowerment of its members. It states:

> We are capable and Competent, Caring and Compassionate, always willing to help another, bonded together in overcoming our addictions" (Women for Sobriety, WFS Motto, 1988).

These philosophy statements guide day-to-day management and program development. For example, Women's Suburban Clinic's feminist statement reads:

> As a feminist clinic, Women's Suburban Clinic is committed to treating the staff with the same respect it gives clients. Women's Suburban Clinic is committed to participatory management, to equitable compensation for the staff and to providing staff with the opportunity for growth and self knowledge. The philosophy guides pregnancy testing, all phases of counseling, options counseling…(Women's Suburban Clinic, Philosophy Statement, 1987).

Advocating for women's rights is another avenue by which these organizations continue to exercise their founding feminist principles. Advocacy on the part of the Domestic Abuse Project to raise public awareness of the incidence of domestic violence in its community by means of a community education newsletter is one example. WOAR staffers took to the streets to hand out information about preventing sexual assault in response to public concern over a series of assaults in Center City in 1988 in March 1988, WOAR publicly challenged a State Representative's remarks about not being able to get pregnant as a result of being raped; and, in May 1988, WOAR convened a meeting of activists to plan Philadelphia's second Take Back the Night March in which over three thousand people marched to demand freedom from physical and economic violence (WOAR, WOARPATH, Summer, 1989).

In addition, all of the 15 organizations studied have joined forces with other pro-choice activists to fight for continued legalized abortion. Organizations like Women's Suburban Clinic and WOAR have recently sponsored trips to Harrisburg, Pennsylvania and Washington, D.C. for pro-choice rallies.

The Valuing of Process By Organization Members

Although the 15 organizations studied are concerned with task accomplishment, there is effort on the part of organizations leaders to emphasize valuing the process as well as concern for end results. Concern for the processes of establishing new policies, developing supporting documentation for new programs, and resolving conflict among staff within these organizations is evident. For example, in the Fall of 1989, the Domestic Abuse Project began an outreach project to offer its free services to a target community within Delaware County. As the project develops, every step will be recorded. The resulting process manual will be shared with other organizations as a model for decentralization of services to victims of domestic violence. In this way, the process, which is of value in and of itself, is captured through the formalized procedure of developing a manual.

A grievance procedure was developed and written in 1988 by the Board of Directors of A Woman's Place coinciding with their problems with a newly hired Executive Director's short-lived tenure and subsequent resignation (B. Frantz, personal communication, November 20, 1989). Before the Board of Directors of the Domestic Abuse Project instituted a change in sick leave policy, discussion with staff took place so that staff input was a part of the decision-making process (M. Bailey, personal communication, August 23, 1989).

Staff meetings are used to air conflicts among staff, to express frustrations about the job, and to obtain new ideas for program development. Almost half of the 15 organizations studied do not currently record staff meeting minutes. By not taking minutes at staff meetings, the experience of the staff meeting process is valued rather than its written preservation.

Characteristics of Current Managers of Feminist Organizations

Leaders of feminist organizations have personal qualities different from leaders of other alternative and traditional organizations. The primary difference is their strong personal connection to feminism. For instance, the new Executive of A Women's Place is formerly the Executive of a rape center in California; the new executive of Women In Transition has worked within Philadelphia's women's movement since the 1970's; and the new Executive of the Domestic Abuse Project has a strong feminist base. One organization currently searching for a new Executive expects the successful candidate to be pro-choice. Five of the organizations still have as the current Executive Director an original Executive Director or a founder.

Another characteristic of current organizational leaders is the importance they place on developing their own management skills. For example, the new Executive Director at A Women's Place feels her previous management experience has better prepared her for her current position (B. Webber, personal communication, October 26, 1989). The Executive Director at Women's Center in Montgomery County just completed a non-profit management training course and is interested in attending additional management training to enhance her management abilities as the organization moves from a volunteer model to a paid staff model (D. Byrne, personal communication, September 6, 1989).

Alongside of this concern for increased management skills is the concern of current organization leaders to manage in accordance with feminist principle. This is illustrated by the management of WOAR which is guided by its 1981 statement on Power and Empowerment:

> WOAR's goal of empowering women to gain control over their lives means that as an organization we must make available to the women who comprise WOAR: a) information; b) opportunities for participation; c) support necessary to enable them to help WOAR achieve its objectives; and d) support necessary to grow in their ability to act on their own behalf in the world (WOAR. Power and Empowerment, 1981).

The integration of feminist principles into management decisions is the management style exercised by 13 of the 15 organizational leaders studied here. This type of management style is referred to as feminist management (B. Webber, personal communication, October 26, 1989). Organizational leaders are sensitive to the feelings of those affected by their decisions. When the decision was made by the current Executive Director and Board of Directors of The Women's Center to staff each location with paid staff instead of volunteers, the Executive Director offered eligible volunteers working at each location the opportunity to become paid. In addition to this organization's move to a paid staff model from a volunteer model, the opening of two branch offices created divisiveness among organizations members. These issues are addressed by the Executive Director in her day-to-day management. For example, she rotates staff meetings among the three locations in response to a developing "we-they" feeling expressed by those not located at the main office. She encourages Board members to volunteer on committees composed of other volunteers and paid staff. In this way, different organizational members work together to complete identified goals.

Conclusion

In summary, although feminist organizations have changed over time from their original alternative organizational forms, dimensions that distinguish them from traditional bureaucratic organizations are present in today's feminist organizations.

Chapter Six reviews and discusses the key findings of this research study. It then draw implication from this study for social work practice and future research.

Chapter 6

Discussions and Implications

Introduction

This dissertation has identified six dimensions which describe the unique alternative forms of feminist organizations at inception. These unique alternative forms reflect feminist principles which guided the development of feminist organizations in the early and mid-seventies. This dissertation has identified and described organizational changes along these dimensions in a sample of feminist organizations. Organizational theorists Katz and Kahn (1978) and Zald and Ash Garner (1987) propose that, over time, alternative organizations change to resemble traditional, bureaucratic organizations. This theoretical perspective led to the formulation of seven research questions focusing on changes, over time, along the six identified dimensions: goals, authority structure, division of labor, personal relationships, rewards and formalization. By examining, through descriptive analysis, changes, over time, in these six dimensions, this dissertation contributes to the literature on organizational evolution, particularly with respect to feminist organizations. This research was intended to answer the following questions: Have feminist organizations become more like bureaucratic organizations? More specifically: Can current organizational forms of feminist organizations support the feminist principles upon which they were founded? Can current organizational forms of feminist organizations still be considered feminist (vehicles for empowerment and social change)? Can the changes in feminist organizations provide a model for the organizational development of other subsets of alternative organizations?

Review and Discussion of Key Research Findings

Goals

Findings for the 15 feminist organizations studied here reveal that 13 of the 15 organizations have retained their original client service goals. For those eight organizations that explicitly defined social change goals as well as client service goals at inception, these social change goals have been retained as well. Both client service and social change goals have directed organizational activity throughout the life cycle, specifically toward continued program expansion for female client populations.

Two of the 15 organizations displaced their original client service goals in favor of new more inclusive goal statements, which took them away from exclusive emphasis on the service needs of women. However, the goal emphasis of the other 13 organizations did not change over time. The eight organizations that had stated social change goals at inception have continued to emphasize these goals. Thirteen of the 15 organizations studied still emphasize their original client service goals.

This finding does not conform to the Weber-Michels model which, according to Zald and Ash Garner (1987), predicts that, over time, the goals of social movement organizations transform toward greater conservatism (the accommodation of organization goals to the dominant societal consensus). Only two of the organizations in this study deliberately redefined their goals in order to accommodate funding sources.

Consistent with the finding of this study is the finding of Hooyman and Cunningham (1986) that, for the 70 national women's organizations they surveyed,

> Although most of the organizations did not explicitly state a goal of changing current structural conditions, they nevertheless view themselves as alternatives to existing systems and therefore as changing the underlying conditions faced by women (p. 174).

Current leaders of 13 of the 15 organizations in this study expressed a similar attitude, using as an example their personal and/or organizations' pro-choice activities.

Formalization

At inception, all of the 15 organizations studied developed either a brochure, a flyer or an information pamphlet for distribution. These communication documents raised public awareness about the organization and its concerns. In addition, distribution of brochures and information pamphlets increased membership and funding opportunities.

At inception, formalized procedure and policy manuals existed in only two of the 15 organizations studied. The two health organizations providing medical services from startup had formal policy and procedure manuals supporting provision of medical services. All 15 organizations studied have increased formalization of their documentation. Ten of the non-medical organizations increased formalization when funding sources required documentation of job descriptions, procedure and policy manuals and organizational charts. In addition, over time, Boards of Directors in all 15 organizations emphasized formalization of organizational documentation.

This research finding confirms that development of formalization in feminist organizations is similar to that seen in other alternative organizations. Riger (1984) identified that as Feminist Movement Organizations aged, formalization increased.

The established of formalized procedures and policies began with recording of information contained in minutes of Board meetings, which formed the core repository of information reflecting decisions by organizational leaders. This purpose of formalizing policies and procedures conforms to the Weber model of bureaucracy, as formalization provides for these organizations a

> well ordered system of rules and procedures that regulate the conduct of work. Rules serve several purposes: (a) They standardize operations and decisions; (b) They serve standardize operations and decisions; (c) They protect incumbents and ensure equality of treatment (Jackson and Moss, 1978, p. 73).

Today, feminist organizations plan ahead of time to record the development of new programs as models for other feminist organizations. For example, in the Fall of 1989, the Domestic Abuse Project began an outreach project; as the project develops, every step will be recorded. The resulting process manual will be shared with other organizations (Hushion, 1990). In this way the process, which is of value in and of itself, is captured through the formalized procedure of developing a manual.

Personal Relationships

All 15 organizations studied evolved from the founders' personal relationships with one another. Some women met while attending consciousness-raising or other women's support groups, while other women already knew each other and joined together to address their mutual shared concerns for specific issues. At inception, professional credentials were unimportant for those working for the organization. More important was the organization member's loyalty and moral commitment to the cause.

This study confirms that personal relationships have continued to play an important role in feminist organizations. Currently, at least 13 of the 15 organizations have hired as leaders women who are committed to feminist principles, as evidenced by their previous work in feminist organizations. In addition, of the 17 original organization members interviewed by the research, nine are still currently connected to their original organization. Six of these nine are either current executive directors or current board presidents of the organization.

However, over time, as these organizations have become more formal, they have also become more impersonal. Increased impersonality in hiring practices and an increased concern for task accomplishment characterizes the development of these organizations. This coincided with organizational growth and funding source requirements of professionalization of management and counseling positions. Job requirements for key organizational positions, such as executive directors and clinical counselors, now have educational and management requirements attached to them.

Professionalism adds credibility to service delivery and makes these organizations more competitive with traditional organizations in seeking funding. In addition, the initial homogenous base of the founders has been broadened, particularly on the Boards of Directors. Diversification of Board members from like-minded individuals to broaden community and business representation has been deliberate on the part of organizational leaders in order to enhance opportunities for funding and widen community support for the organizations.

The combination of personal and impersonal qualities currently found in feminist organizations has created some conflict in ownership and power, primarily between volunteers and paid staff. Implications of this finding are discussed in the next section.

Rewards

For all 15 organizations studied, initial reward systems were composed of purposive and friendship rewards. Seven of the 15 organizations began as all-volunteer organizations with no material rewards provided. A shift to include material rewards in the reward systems of these seven all-volunteer organizations occurred over time. For the other eight organizations with paid staff at inception, as well as the seven original all-volunteer organizations, increased pay differentials among staff based on credentials and/or experience is now the norm.

For all 15 organizations studied, the reward systems have become multifaceted including material, purposive, friendship and personal rewards. Synonymous with this study's findings regarding the movement toward impersonal intraorganizational relationships, material rewards are now a part of the reward systems of all these organizations. This finding conforms to Katz and Kahn's (1978) systems theory of specialization that differential pay is a further implication of specialization. Competition with traditional and other feminist organizations for professional staff occurs, suggesting that current leaders of feminist organizations must pay attention to offering desirable salaries and benefits which will attract qualified individuals.

The role of the volunteer is now significantly different from the original voluntary role both in status and function. Volunteers in the organizations still using them no longer work alongside paid staff, but are used to supplement paid staff. The rewards are also less clear for current volunteers. Findings indicate that volunteers are given priority in hiring for salaried positions. Because of the change in the role of volunteers, for those who do not desire to become paid employees, opportunities for intrinsic rewards are less apparent in today's feminist organizations. This may be why "oldtimers" complain that newer volunteers lack commitment and dedication the oldtimers had (B. Sayre, personal communication, November 10, 1989). This finding is consistent with Newman's (1980) finding that, as older volunteers became salaried staff, newer volunteers entered the organization without the benefit of experiencing others' personal relationships as an existing reward of the organization.

Division of Labor

Eight of the 15 organizations studied had no formalized differentiation of labor among organization members at inception. For the seven other organizations, job differentiation was based on the organization members' areas of interest and/or expertise.

In all 15 organizations studied, job specialization increased as the organizations aged. This finding is consistent with the finding of Epstein, Russell and Silvern (1988) that, as battered women's shelters develop, more reliance on paid labor for specialized roles occurs. This finding of increased specialization as organizations age fits into Katz and Kahn's systems theory of specialization which explains specialization in bureaucratic organizations.

Differential job titles that accompany specialization formalize the expertise of individual members. This formalization of expertise is a natural developmental progression legitimizing the growth of technical competence of individual staff members. The two major areas in which specialization has grown are management and delivery of clinical services. This specialization delineates the organization into horizontal and vertical differentiation, creating unequal power among organization members.

Authority Structure

Eight of the 15 organizations studied began as collectives with no formal authority structure other than the authority residing in the collective. For the other seven organizations, founders of these organizations made conscious decisions to structure their organizations as hierarchies, albeit with little distance from top to bottom. Over time, in all eight collectives, the collective structure gave way to some degree of a hierarchical structure. Centralized decision-making rather than consensual decision-making accompanied this movement to a hierarchical structure. Centralized decision-making rather than consensual decision-making accompanied this movement to a hierarchical structure. Now, in all 15 organizations studied, hierarchies exist. Each of the 15 organizations currently has a chain of command which legitimizes authority of some over others.

Unlike the finding of Hooyman and Cunningham (1986) that

> most of the organizations expressed a commitment to both a consensual organizational style and the elimination of positions of power through collective decision making (p. 176).

The organizations in this study make no such claim. A finding of this study reveals that, for all 15 organizations, decision-making power resides with a single person or a group of individuals positioned at the top of the hierarchy.

The larger organizations in this study added hierarchical layers at the top, with the intent of separating administrative tasks from direct services. This finding is consistent with Katz and Kahn's (1978) systems of theory of specialization that, as job specialization increases, centralized decision-making occurs. In this way, feminist organizations have developed similarly to bureaucratic organizations.

Summary of Key Findings of This Research Study

1. Those feminist organizations in this study with social change goals at inception have retained their social change goals.

2. Two of the 15 feminist organizations displaced their feminist client service goals to meet funding criteria. The other 13 organizations studied have retained original client service goals.

3. Over time, all 15 organizations have become more formalized, more impersonal, more specialized and hierarchical. These changes are associated with organizational growth, increased requirements by funding

sources, and changes in organizational leadership.

4. For all 15 organizations, a hierarchical authority chain of command currently exists.

5. Over time, the original role of the volunteer as counselor has been replaced by paid professional staff. Volunteer relationships with paid staff are strained with regard to ownership of the organization and decision-making power.

Implications for Social Work Practice

One implication for social work practice drawn from the findings of this study is that practitioners in feminist organizations are exposed to organizational factors that research supports can contribute to burnout (Cherniss and Krantz, 1983; Scully, 1983; Pines and Aronson, 1988).

These factors include: 1) feminist organizations are high intensity organizations with unclear boundaries between personal and professional identities; 2) practitioners in feminist organizations involve themselves in activities, focused on feminist issues, extending beyond the work day; and, 3) feminist organizations are composed of a homogenous population.

Practitioners in feminist organizations often work as advocates for feminist causes in addition to their primary job responsibilities. They feel responsible, as women, to advocate for all women's issues. They attend rallies promoting feminist causes. They attend conferences focusing on women's issues and do volunteer work for different feminist organizations. One women worked at Women In Transition, was a Board member of another feminist organization, and volunteered at yet another feminist organization. This is the rule, not the exception (R. Hacker, personal communication, September 29, 1989). In addition, they are members of multiple social and political feminist organizations. All of the 15 organizations in this study currently have organization members active in abortion rights organizations. Other organizations that practitioners belong to are national women's rights organizations as well as educational and professional women's organizations.

Practitioners in feminist organizations feel obligated to disseminate their expertise to other practitioners through speaking engagements, publications, conference organizing and attendance. WOAR has sponsored one national conference a year a well as many local workshops. Feminist organizations jointly sponsor frequent state and local conferences (K. Kulp, personal communication, August 29, 1989).

Related research by Cherniss and Krantz (1983) on organizations with an ideological base supports organizational homogeneity contributing to burnout. Their research (Cherniss and Krantz, 1983), on Montesorri schools suggests that lack of tolerance of other viewpoints lead to stagnation, lack of creativity and innovation. In addition, Cherniss and Krantz (1983) found that over commitment to an ideology may become the sole organizational objective overshadowing an organization's clinical objectives without the members realizing this is occurring.

Related research on organizational factors contributing to burnout in other human service organizations suggests that:

> the interpenetration of life and work is one of the most significant occupational problems faced by the worker dealing with emotionally evocative experiences (Pines and Aronson, 1988, p. 86).

In addition, like practitioners in feminist organizations, practitioners in human service organizations have a client-centered orientation in which the needs of the clients dictate the practitioner's role. "In many of these professions, work is seen not as a job but as a calling..." (Pines and Aronson, 1988, p. 88).

Managers of feminist and other human service organizations with similar organizational characteristics, who acknowledge the possibility of worker burnout, may want to develop organizational tactics addressing burnout. One suggestion growing out of the findings of this study as well as from the literature on burnout in human service organizations (Scully, 1983; Pines and Aronson, 1988) is developing practitioner support groups. Support groups focus on work-related issues providing a safe place for practitioners to share feelings about their work-related experiences (Scully, 1983). Support groups are a vehicle for practitioners to receive support from other practitioners (Scully, 1983). The functioning of support groups varies according to the needs and objectives of the group (Scully, 1983). Practitioners in feminist organizations will want to develop support groups consistent with feminist ideology. Rotating group leaders, emphasizing process, and flexible agendas growing out of the support group meetings are characteristics of support groups in accordance with feminist ideology. Organizational leaders' acceptance of practitioners; support groups by allotting time during the work day, making available a private room, and prohibiting management interference can contribute to reducing practitioner burnout in all human service organizations.

Another suggestion drawn from the literature (Pines and Aronson, 1988) is making available to practitioners by organization leaders of "times out".

As defined by Pines and Aronson (1988):

> 'times out' are…not merely short breaks from work such as rest periods or
> coffee breaks. Rather, they are opportunities for the staff members to choose
> some less stressful work while other staff take over their more stressful
> responsibilities (p. 189).

In human service organizations, direct contact with clients is associated with the highest levels of burnout (Pines and Aronson, 1988). "Times out" require the receptivity of organizational leaders to providing practitioners with the opportunity to work in in-direct services (conference planning, speaking engagements and training) while reducing time spent in direct services. Freedom to experience a variety of jobs may help practitioners select preferences in work assignments thus contributing to their continued job satisfaction (Pines and Aronson, 1988).

Staff meetings are one organizational buffer used in feminist organizations confronting practitioner burnout. Research by Pines and Aronson (1988) supports the use of staff meetings as a place where workers can discuss problems and complaints. In eight of the 15 organizations studied, minutes of staff meetings are not kept. In these organizations, staff can blow off steam and air feelings at staff meetings. Pines and Aronson (1988) suggest restating staff complaints as positive recommendations for implementing by management (Pines and Aronson, 1988).

Another practice implication of the research reported here is the engagement of clients of human service organizations in advocacy work. This implication addresses the lack of power felt by clients of feminist and other human service organizations. One technique for client empowerment suggested by these findings is advocacy work by clients.

According to Gutierrez (1990):

> the process of empowerment occurs on the individual, interpersonal, and
> institutional levels, where, the person develops a sense of personal
> power…and an ability to work with others to change social institutions (p.
> 150).

Social work practitioners may be aware of how lack of power affects clients, but lack of techniques of how to empower them (Gutierrez, 1990). Advocacy work by clients is an activity supporting their empowerment (Solomon, 1981).

Educating clients regarding the social, political and legal circumstances affecting their situations is a first step towards advocacy work by clients. Feminist organizations such as the Domestic Abuse Project show clients how to file legal documents themselves (Domestic Abuse Project, Newsletter of Domestic Abuse Project, Winter, 1990).

Feminist organizations provide vehicles for the mutual education of clients and practitioners by continual sharing of information through conference attendance and joint workshops with other feminist organizations. The Domestic Abuse Project's support group, Survivors for Formerly Battered Women, provides former clients a forum in which they can collectively advocate (Domestic Abuse Project, Newsletter of Domestic Abuse Project, Fall, 1986). Solomon (1981) refers to consciousness raising which allows

> women the opportunity to explore with other women issues related to their personal and collective identities or to relate these identities to the larger political and economic world (p. 211).

These organizations encourage clients to move this new knowledge from the individual level to the institutional level by becoming activists for feminist causes. For example, a former Domestic Abuse Project client was elected state chair of the Formerly Battered Women's Caucus of the Pennsylvania Coalition Against Domestic Violence. WOAR organization members and clients joined together to march to Washington, D.C. and to Harrisburg, Pennsylvania in 1989 to fight for continued legalized abortion (WOAR, WOARPATH, Summer, 1989). Women's Suburban Clinic staffers and clients have protested together against legislation restricting abortions and have supported each other's right to enter the clinic against the protests of pro-lifers (S. Hollos, personal communication, August 2, 1989). Women In Transition (WIT) published a trainer's manual written jointly by clients and practitioners (Women In Transition, A Facilitator's Guide to Working with Separated and Divorced Women, 1982).

Over time, former clients have become paid staff in many feminist organizations. For instance, a former client of Domestic Abuse Project became the organization's fiscal coordinator. Women In Transition began hiring clients in the position of temporary work internships providing them a supportive work situation and a recent work reference (Women In Transition, WIT Annual Report, 1986).

The findings of this study suggest that managers of feminist organizations practice a unique form of management which they have termed feminist management. Feminist management combines those management skills necessary for managing bureaucratic structures with a personal commitment to feminist principles. The findings of this study indicate that one way this feminist commitment impacts on bureaucratic management style is that feminist managers differ in their style of decision-making from managers in traditional bureaucratic organizations. Feminist managers emphasize and value the decision-making process itself, involve organization members on various hierarchical levels in the decision-making process, and are sensitive to the feelings of those organization members affected by management decisions. These three ingredients in the decision-making process emphasize communication among organization members in feminist organizations.

The implication for managers in other human service organizations is that employment of this feminist management style in traditional bureaucratic organizations may encourage increased communication across hierarchical levels. For example, the Board of Directors of Domestic Abuse Project made adjustments to its sick leave policy after thorough discussions with the entire staff. Even so, changes in the sick leave policy left some of the staff feeling disempowered. The Executive Director of Domestic Abuse Project sensitive to this overall staff feeling, encouraged small group discussions by staff (M. Bailey, personal communication, August 23, 1989).

Feminist management encourages the fullest participation of all organizations members. For example, managers of WOAR have attempted to integrate feminist principles into that organization's bureaucratic organizational structure by employing a "Power and Empowerment" conceptual framework from which to view its formal hierarchical structure. This Power and Empowerment framework states that:

> WOAR has a formal power structure which depends for its effectiveness on widespread participation by the entire membership: 1) The Board of Directors has been empowered by the membership to set organizational policy, oversee the work of the organization, hire and fire the Executive Director...2) The Executive Director has been empowered by the Board to hire and fire staff, raise funds...and administer the organization within certain guidelines (such as striving for consensus with committee and staff involved in specific issues)...3) Programs and Committees have been empowered by the Board to participate in developing organizational objectives...(WOAR, Power and Empowerment, 1981).

WOAR's "Power and Empowerment" statement suggests a cone-like hierarchy which integrates the feminist principles of empowerment and process within a hierarchical structure. Figure 6.1 represents this unique hierarchical model. The flow of information and accountability in this model is open and fluid, facilitating dialogue across all levels. This unique hierarchical model is consistent with a systems perspective of organizations (Gordon, 1987). The organization, as a system, is composed of persons or groups of persons who interact and influence each other's behavior and are interdependent (Gordon, 1987). This perspective views feedback as a key characteristic of any system which this model supports.

For instance, Domestic Abuse Project's community outreach program targeted to a specific area of Delaware County is a result of communication between Domestic Abuse Project organization members and the community. Women's Center of Montgomery County developed its two branch offices out of expressed community concern. In addition, this organization moved from a volunteer to a paid staff model in an attempt to deliver more consistent professional services to clients. This change-over required communication among all hierarchical levels so that feelings of all involved were listened to and taken into consideration when decisions had to be made.

The fourth implication drawn from the findings of this study is the need for Board of Directors to develop written policy addressing the extent to which human service organizations will alter, expand or change original organizational goals in order to obtain new funding sources. Evidence from this study indicates that, when feminist organizations have allowed opportunities for funding to dictate changes in organizational goals, these organizations have experienced conflict among practitioners as well as loss of commitment by staff.

For example, in order to secure its tenuous financial position, Women In Transition (WIT) obtained funds for a drug and alcohol program by extending its original goal of serving separated and divorced women to include all women in transition. With the new funds, WIT was required to hire practitioners utilizing a different counseling model from those already employed by WIT. This created divisiveness between these two groups leading to complaints of discrimination, and eventual resignations.

In another instance, Women's Resource Center began programs based on the availability of new funds which were short-lived as were the new programs created by them. Practitioners in this organization were laid off and clients attached to these short-lived programs were shifted to programs with different purposes and practitioners. Remaining practitioners felt demoralized, were spread thinly across programs and volunteers replaced practitioners escalating conflict between these two groups regarding ownership of the organization (S. Staas, personal communication, December 4, 1989).

Board of Directors are responsible for establishing the direction of the organization as guided by its goals. Clarity in the organization's purpose strengthens and sustains practitioner's commitment which is a deterrent

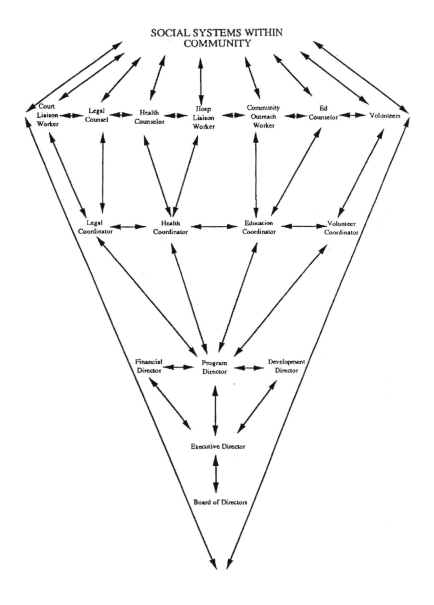

Figure 6.1. An Empowerment Hierarchy

to burnout (Cherniss and Krantz, 1983).

Implications for Further Research

The findings of this study have implications for four areas in which to focus future research.

1. The first area for future research suggested by the findings of this study is an intensive examination of how differences in organizational development in a subset of feminist organizations, rape crisis centers, has influenced the effectiveness of services to victims of rape and sexual assault and their communities. The findings of this study suggest that there may be a difference between those rape crisis organizations that did not transform into comprehensive victims service centers and those that did in delivery of service, community outreach, and education. Differences among the organizations initially established for the same purpose can be thoroughly examined by a statewide study of the organization members of the Pennsylvania Coalition Against Rape (PCAR). Differences between organizations that have remained focused on the rape crisis cause and those organizations that have transformed into comprehensive victims service centers can be evaluated with respect to service delivery effectiveness to rape and sexual assault victims and the availability of educational and other preventative services intended to raise community awareness and decrease the incidence of rape and sexual assault in communities.

In addition, an analysis of the organizational development of the Coalition (PCAR) as a collection of organizations with different developmental histories will provide more information regarding overall effectiveness of services and the contribution each type of organization has made in this effort.

2. The findings of this study suggest further research of the similarities and differences in the evolution of the roles of volunteers in feminist and traditional organizations. One of the key findings of this study was that, over time, the original roles of volunteer in feminist organizations have been displaced by paid professional staff. The findings of this study imply that, over time, volunteers in feminist organizations lose ownership of the organization and become disempowered, leading to strained relationships with paid staff members.

This proposed research will compare and contrast the growth and development of utilization of volunteers in traditional and feminist organizations, how they are currently utilized by each type of organization, and the factors that influence the status and power of volunteers within each type of organization. This proposed research is relevant for recruitment and retention of volunteers in a variety of organizations.

3. Two of the organizations studied here, Domestic Abuse Project and WOAR, are experimenting with decentralized services in order to increase outreach and service delivery to targeted community areas. Leaders of these two organizations anticipate that decentralized services will increase the number of staff members involved in decision-making on a day-to-day basis, improve community awareness and community involvement, and increase opportunities for societal change, such as the decline in the incidence of rape (K. Kulp, personal communication, August 29, 1989). Evaluation of the effectiveness of the decentralized model used by these two organizations determine the feasibility for the model's future replication by feminist and other organizations. In addition, evaluation of the effectiveness of the decentralized model will support future funding for these projects.

4. The finding of this study that original organizational goals can be retained while new structures are developed that support these original goals has implications for further research on the organizational development of other feminist research on the organizational development of other feminist and non-traditional organizations growing out of social movements. One of the limitations of this study is that the case study methodology prevents generalizing to other subsets of feminist organizations or to subsets of other alternative organizations. Additional research documenting this phenomenon is important to further clarify a model of organizational development for those organizations that are founded as alternatives to traditional organizations.

Another limitation of the case study method is that it is not amenable to quantitative analysis so that relationships of cause ad effect remain undetermined. In particular, future use of a different design which allows a quantitative approach would be invaluable to further substantiate the relationships among organization characteristics along critical dimensions and the influence of funding sources, organizational growth, leadership changes, and interorganizational relationships on organizational form. One suggestions growing out of the implications of this study design is to survey a larger geographical area of feminist organizations by questionnaire regarding the priorities that determine changes in characteristics of the six organizational dimensions. These priorities could include relationships with funding sources, interorganizational growth. These would serve as the independent variables while the six organizational dimensions would be dependent variables in this proposed future study. Such a study will help leaders of feminist organizations safeguard feminist principles as further changes in organizational structure occur, as influenced by the independent variables.

Conclusion

The emphasis of this study has been on changes, over time, in feminist organizations. This study has shown that these organizations have changed from alternative forms to bureaucratic organizational forms while retaining original goals within an organizational structure that has become more hierarchical and more impersonal with greater job specialization. In addition, current organizational leaders and managers have integrated feminist principles into their management styles, allowing them to retain and continue to promote significant feminist principles.

APPENDIX A

Diane Metzendorf, ACSW
450F Montgomery Ave.
Haverford, PA 19041
649-5749

July 19, 1989

Dear   :

I am currently competing my doctorate in social work at the University of Pennsylvania. The research that I would like your organization to be a part of is the last step in this process. As an introduction to research, I am outlining for you: a) the purpose of my research; b. what dimensions of feminist organizations I will be looking at and; c. How I will gather my data at each feminist organization.

In addition, I have attached an agreement statement. Please feel free to amend this statement as you deem applicable to your organization.

The purpose of my research is to describe how feminist organizations have changed since their inception ten or more years ago. The literature on feminist organizations identifies those feminist organizations beginning in the seventies as having an alternative organizational form (different from the bureaucratic organizational form of traditional human service organizations) which reflected the feminist ideology of the women's movement of the seventies. By doing this research, I hope to answer the questions: To what extend have feminist organizations changed from their alternative organizational forms of the seventies? And; What do feminist organizations look like as mature organizations?

In order to answer these questions, I am studying twenty (20) feminist service organizations which were begun in the seventies by women for women in the five county area (Bucks, Philadelphia, Chester, Montgomery and Delaware). I will be aggregating my findings on the data collected at the twenty (20) organizations.

I will be studying the following six dimensions of feminist organizations: goals; authority structure; division of labor; social relations; rewards; and formalization at two points in time (year 1 and this current year). In addition, I will be looking at the factors that are associated with change in these dimensions such as leadership changes, growth in size, program development and professionalism and funding source changes.

In order to determine the extent to which feminist organizations have changed on each dimension, I have developed a checklist for each dimension which documents the degree to which each dimension existed at the two points in time (year 1 and current year).

So that I may collect the above data, it is necessary for me to examine archival and current documents of each feminist organization. These documents include but are not limited to: incorporation papers; original and current mission statements; job descriptions, organizational charts; board meeting minutes; etc. In addition, I have developed a brief questionnaire to administer to one of the founders and to the current executive director of each feminist organization. I will write a brief biography of each feminist organization highlighting major events in the organization's life history.

I am very excited about my research and hope that your organization will join me in my efforts to document the growth of feminist organizations as mature, viable feminist organizations. I will e contacting you at the beginning of next week so that we can set up a time to meet. Thank you for your support.

Sincerely,

Diane Metzendorf, ACSW

APPENDIX B

AGREEMENT TO COOPERATE IN STUDY

I, _____ agree that _____
   Representative of Org.   Name of Organization

Will cooperate with Diane Metzendorf, researcher, in participating in the study of feminist organizations.

This agreement permits Ms. Metzendorf to interiew the current Executive Director, one founder or other historian, ad to examine the archival documents and current documents.

In return, _____ asks that Ms. Metzendorf,
              Name of Organization

respect the following request of _____ :
                                Name of Organization

Signed _____ (Researcher)

Signed _____ (Rep. of Org.)

Date _____

For researcher use only

Date Organization Began Operating _____

Number of Incorporators _____

Number of Women Incorporators _____

APPENDIX C

STRUCTURED INTERVIEW GUIDE
FOR INTERVIEW WITH FOUNDER
AND EXECUTIVE DIRECTOR

Questions on Goal Emphasis

1. In your (Name of Document), your agency listed the following goals (read them). Would you say these accurately reflect the goals of your organization as they (stood the first year of your existence) now stand or are there other goals you see as equally important?

	Important		Type of Goal
Goal	**YES**	**NO**	**Soc change/client ser**
1			
2			
3			
4			
5			
6			

2. What other goals (were) are not listed but are important?

Goal	**Type of goal (sc/cs)**
1	
2	
3	
4	
5	

Are the following documents distributed by the leadership? (A document is at minimum a single piece of paper with printed, typed or otherwise reproduced content – not handwritten) and if so, to whom?

Information Handbook ____Yes ____ No Distributed to what proportion of the staff?

____ 0%

____ 1%-24%

____ 25%-50%

____ 51%-75%

____ 76%-100%

Personnel Manual ____Yes ____ No Distributed to what proportion of the staff?
____ 0%
____ 1%-24%
____ 25%-50%
____ 51%-75%
____ 76%-100%

Procedures manual ____Yes ____ No Distributed to what proportion of the staff?
____ 0%
____ 1%-24%
____ 25%-50%
____ 51%-75%
____ 76%-100%

Job Descriptions ____Yes ____ No Distributed to what proportion of the staff?
____ 0%
____ 1%-24%
____ 25%-50%
____ 51%-75%
____ 76%-100%

Staff meeting minutes ____Yes ____ No Distributed to what proportion of the staff?
____ 0%
____ 1%-24%
____ 25%-50%
____ 51%-75%
____ 76%-100%

Organizational Chart ____Yes ____ No Distributed to what proportion of the staff?
____ 0%
____ 1%-24%
____ 25%-50%
____ 51%-75%
____ 76%-100%

Questions On Division of Labor

(Was there) Is there any rotation of jobs among staff?

___Yes ___No

About what percent of the staff participate in job rotation?
___ 100%
___ 75%
___ 50%
___ 25%
___ 0%

Questions On Authority Structure

Decisions on hiring new staff – who participates

	Yes	No
All hierarchical levels	___	___
Only the lowest nonprofessional hierarchical level does not participate	___	___
Only professional hierarchical levels and above	___	___
Only administrative hierarchical levels and above	___	___
Only executive hierarchical levels	___	___

Decisions On Promoting Staff – Who Participates

	Yes	No
All hierarchical levels	___	___
Only the lowest nonprofessional hierarchical level does not participate	___	___
Only professional hierarchical levels and above	___	___
Only administrative hierarchical levels and above	___	___
Only executive hierarchical levels	___	___

Decisions On Adoption of New Policies – Who Participates

	Yes	No
All hierarchical levels	___	___
Only the lowest nonprofessional hierarchical level does not participate	___	___
Only professional hierarchical levels and above	___	___
Only administrative hierarchical levels and above	___	___
Only executive hierarchical levels	___	___

Decisions On Adoptions of New Programs – Who Participates

	Yes	No
All hierarchical levels	___	___
Only the lowest nonprofessional hierarchical level does not participate	___	___
Only professional hierarchical levels and above	___	___
Only administrative hierarchical levels and above	___	___
Only executive hierarchical levels	___	___

Questions On Social Relations

What percent of the total staff population knew each other due to belonging to the same feminist organizations (this includes volunteers) before coming to work at this organization?

___ Very many
___ Many
___ Some
___ Few
___ Very few

Are (were) agency personnel encouraged to join feminist organizations outside of work?

___ Very strongly encouraged
___ Strongly encouraged
___ Somewhat encouraged
___ Slightly encouraged
___ Not at all encouraged

Is there socializing outside of work among agency personnel?

___ Very often
___ Often
___ Occasionally
___ Almost never
___ Never

Questions On Rewards
What is the rate of turnover in your organization for the following groups of agency personnel?

Volunteers
—— Very low
—— Low
—— Moderate
—— High
—— Very high

Non-professionals
—— Very low
—— Low
—— Moderate
—— High
—— Very high

Professionals
—— Very low
—— Low
—— Moderate
—— High
—— Very high

Administrators
—— Very low
—— Low
—— Moderate
—— High
—— Very high

Executive Director
—— Very low
—— Low
—— Moderate
—— High
—— Very high

How competitive are your salary levels with the salary levels of other similar organizations in the community?

—— Not at all competitive

—— Slightly competitive

—— Moderately competitive

—— Competitive

—— Very competitive

APPENDIX D

Forms on which to document type of goal:
ORIGINAL GOALS

(As stated in the organization's statement of incorporation or mission statement, write in the lines below the original goals in their order of priority (if indicated).

SOURCE: _____

DATE OF SOURCE: _____

1. _____

_____

_____

_____

Type of Goal: Social Change _____   **Client Service** _____

2. _____

_____

_____

_____

Type of Goal: Social Change _____   **Client Service** _____

3. _____

_____

_____

_____

Type of Goal: Social Change _____   **Client Service** _____

4. _____

_____

_____

_____

Type of Goal: Social Change _____   **Client Service** _____

5. _____

_____

_____

_____

Type of Goal: Social Change _____   **Client Service** _____

TOTAL SOCIAL CHANGE GOALS: _____
TOTAL CLIENT SERVICE GOALS: _____

CURRENT GOALS

SOURCE: _____

DATE OF SOURCE: _____

1. _____

_____

_____

_____

Type of Goal: Social Change _____   **Client Service** _____

2. _____

_____

_____

_____

Type of Goal: Social Change _____   **Client Service** _____

3. _____

_____

_____

_____

Type of Goal: Social Change _____   **Client Service** _____

4. _____

_____

_____

_____

Type of Goal: Social Change _____   **Client Service** _____

5. _____

_____

_____

_____

Type of Goal: Social Change _____ **Client Service** _____

TOTAL SOCIAL CHANGE GOALS: _____
TOTAL CLIENT SERVICE GOALS: _____

APPENDIX E

DOCUMENTATION OF DEPENDENT VARIABLES

FUNDING RESOURCES

	YES	NO	AMT (if possible)	% of Total
Resources				
EXTERNAL				
Gov't.				
Fed				
State				
Local				
PrFound				
UW				
WW				
Pri Cont				
UJA				
TOTAL				
INTERNAL				
MemDues				
FeeServ				
Fundraise				
SpeakFee				
LitFee				
TOTAL				

Interorganizational Relations
# of Referral Agencies
Feminist Organizations _____
Traditional Organizations _____

Number of Agencies Referred to
Feminist Organizations _____
Traditional Organizations _____
# of organizations in the country who offer the same services to the same client population _____

GROWTH   CURRENT YEAR
Size of annual budget
# of total paid staff
# of paid prof staff
# of paid nonprof staff
# of volunteers
# of Bd of Directors
#paid full time staff
#paid part time staff
# of clients served
# of males employed
# of male clients

LEADERSHIP

Total # of Years Exe Dir has worked for this organization

POSITIONS HELD _____ YEARS _____

# of Years Exe Dir has been in current position

If current exec worked elsewhere, did she work for feminist organization previously.   YES ___ NO ___

# of executive directors since founding of organization _____

# of executive directors hired from outside _____

# of executive directors promoted from within _____

REFERENCES

A Woman's Place. (1977, February 7). Articles of Incorporation. (Available from A Women's Place, P.O. Box 229, Doylestown, PA 18901).

A Woman's Place. (1989, Fall). Newsletter of A Woman's Place. (Available from A Woman's Place, P.O. Box 299, Doylestown, PA 18901).

A Woman's Place. (1989). A Woman's Place brochure. (Available from A Woman's Place, P.O. Box 39, Doylestown, PA 18901).

Aldrich, H., & Mueller, S (1982). The evolution of organizational forms: Technology, coordination, and control. Research in Organizational Behavior, 4, 33-87.

Benson, E.S. (1980). Ideology and practice of the women's movement: A case study of a self-help group, a history of Delaware County Marital Abuse Project. Unpublished master's thesis, Lincoln University, Oxford, PA.

Black, N. (1989). Social feminism. Ithaca, NY: Cornell University Press.

Chambless, D. (1980, December 21). Letter to the Feminist Therapy Collective task force. (Available from the Women's Therapy Center, 1930 Chestnut Street, Philadelphia, PA 19106.

Cherniss, C., & Krantz, D. (1983). The ideological community as an antidote to burnout in the human services. In B. Farber (Ed.), Stress and burnout in the human service professions (pp. 198-212). New York: Pergamon.

Collins, B., & Whalen, M. (1989). The rape crisis movement: Radical or reformist? Social Work, 34, 61-63

Davidson, L. 2980). Countercultural organizations and bureaucracy: Limits on the revolution. In J. Freeman (Ed.), Social movements of the 60's and 70's (pp. 211-226). New York: Longman

Deckard, B. S. (1979). The women's movement: Political, socioeconomic, and psychological issues. New York: Harper & Row.

Domestic Abuse Project. (1986). Newsletter of Domestic Abuse Project. (Available from Domestic Abuse Project of Delaware County, Inc., P.O. Box 174, Media, PA 19063.

Domestic Abuse Project. (1989). Organizational chart. (Available from Domestic Abuse Project of Delaware County, Inc., P.O. Box 174, Media, PA 19063).

Elias, S. (1972, November). The Feminist Therapy Collective. Paper presented at Bryn Mawr Graduate School of Social Work and Social Reearch, Bryn Mawr, PA.

Epstein, S., Russel, G., & Silvern, L. (1988). Structure and ideology of shelters for battered women. American Journal of Community Psychology, 16(3), 345-367.

Ferree, M., & Hess, B. (1985). Controversy and coalition: The new feminist movement. Boston: Twayne.

Freeman, J. (1982). Organizational life cycles and natural selection processes. Research in Organizational Behavior, 4, 1-32.

Freeman, J., & Hannan, M. (1983). Niche width and the dynamics of organizational populations. American Journal of Sociology, 88, 1116-1145.

Galper, M., & Washburne, C. (1976). Maximizing he impact of an alternative agency. Journal of Sociology and Social Welfare, 4, 248-257.

Gerth, H. J., & Mills, C. W. (19460. From Max Weber: Essays in sociology. New York: Oxford University Press.

Gordon, J. (1987). A diagnostic approach to organizational behavior (2nd ed.). Boston: Allyn & Bacon.

Gutierrez, L. (1990). Working with women of color: An empowerment perspective. Social Work. 35(2), 149-154.

Hall, R. (1963). The concept of bureaucracy: An empirical assessment. American Journal of Sociology, 69(1), 32-40.

Hall, R. (1972). Organizations: Structure and Process. Englewood Cliffs, NJ: Prentice-Hall.

Hannan, M., & Freeman, J. (1977). The population ecology of organizations. American Journal of Sociology, 82(5), 929-964.

Hannan M., & Freeman, J. (1984). Structural inertia and organizational change. American Sociological Review, 49, 149-164.

Hicks, W. (1977). Report of the Coordinating Office of Drug and Alcohol Abuse Programs. Philadelphia: Coordinating Office of Drug and Alcohol Programs.

Hooyman, N. R., & Cunningham, R. (1986). An alternative administrative style. In N. Van Den Bergh & L. Cooper (Eds.), Feminist Visions for Social Work (pp. 163-186). Silver Springs, MD: NASW.

Hopkins, N. (Undated). Early WRC History. (Available from Women's Resource Center, P.O. Box 309, Wayne, PA 19087).

Humme, E. (1980). Title XX Proposal. (Available from Domestic Abuse Project of Delaware County, Inc., P.O. Box 174, Media, PA 19063).

Hushion, C. (Ed). (1990, Winter). Newsletter of Domestic Abuse Project of Delaware County, Inc. (Available from Domestic Abuse Project of Delaware County, Inc., P.O. Box 174, Media, PA 19063).

Interim House. (1971, August 24). Minutes of Board Meeting. (Available from Interim House, 333 W. Upsal Street, Philadelphia, PA 19119).

Interim House. (1972, August 29). Grant Proposal to the Coordinating Office for Drug and Alcohol Abuse Programs. (Available from Interim House, 333 W. Upsal Street, Philadelphia, PA 19119).

Interim House. (1985). Policy and Procedures Manual. (Available from Interim House, 333 W. Upsal Street, Philadelphia, PA 19119).

Jackson, J., and Morgan, C. (1978). Organization Theory. Englewood Cliffs, NJ: Prentice-Hall.

Johnson, J. (1981). Program enterprise and official cooptation in the battered women's shelter movement. American Behavioral Scientist, 24, 827-842.

Kalton, G. (1987). Introduction To Survey Sampling. Beverly Hills, CA: Sage.

Katz, D., & Kahn, R. (1978). The Social Psychology of Organizations (2nd ed.). New York: Wiley.

Kimberly, J. (1976). Issues in the design of longitudinal organizational research. Sociological Methods & Research, 4,(3), 321-347.

Kimberly, J. (1980). The life cycle analogy and the study of organizations: Introduction. In J. Kimberly, R. Miles & Associates (Eds.), The Organizational Life Cycle (pp. 1-14). San Francisco: Jossey Bass.

Kirkpatrick, J. (1981). Women for Sobriety. In D. Masi (Ed.), Organizing for women (pp. 185-191). Lexington, MA: Lexington.

Marital Abuse Project. (1976). Grant Proposal to the Pennsylvania Governor' Justice Commission. (Available from Domestic Abuse Project of Delaware County, Inc., P.O. Box 174, Media, PA 19063).

McCarthy, J. D., & Zald, M. N. (1987). Resource mobilization and social movements: A partial theory. In M. N. Zlad & J. D. McCarthy (Eds.). Social movements in an organizational society (pp. 121-142). New Brunswick, NJ: Transaction.

McMahon, S. L. (Undated). Coming of age: Management issues in a women's organization. Unpublished manuscript.

McShane, C., & Oliver, J. (1978). Women's groups as alternative human service agencies. Journal of Sociology & Social Welfare, 5(5), 616-626.

Michels, R. (1949). Political parties. Glencoe, IL: Free Press.

Murray, S. (1988). The unhappy marriage of theory and practice: An analysis of a battered women's shelter. NWSA Journal, 1, 75-92.

Newman, K. (1980). Incipient bureaucracy: The development of hierarchies in egalitarian organizations. In G. Britan & D. Cohen (Eds.), Anthropological studies on bureaucracy (pp. 143-163). Philadelphia: Institute for the Study of Human Services.

Oliver, J., & McShane, C. (1979). A survival model for alternative organizations. California Sociologist, 2, 213-221.

Organization tackles female problem drinker. (1976). United Press International.

Perlmutter, F. (1988). Administering alternative social programs. Manuscript submitted for publication.

Pennings, J. (1973). Measures of organizational structure: A methodological note. American Journal of Sociology, 79(3), 686-704.

Philadelphia Women's Network. (Undated). Application for membership. (Available from Philadelphia Women's Network, 513 Valmore Road, Fairless Hills, PA 19030).

Philadelphia Women's Network. (Undated). PWN brochure. (Available from Philadelphia Women's Network, 513 Valmore Road, Fairless Hills, PA 19030).

Pines, A., & Aronson, E. (1988). Career Burnout. New York: The Free Press.

Powell, D. M. (1986). Managing organizational problems in alternative service organizations. Administration in Social Work, 10(3), 57-69.

Price, J. (1972). Handbook of organizational measurement. Lexington, MA: Heath.

Profile of Lyn McMahon. (1987, March 27). University City News.

Pugh, D. S., Hickson, D., Hinings, C., & Turner, C. (1968). Dimensions of organizational structure. Administrative Science Quarterly, 13, 65-105.

Rape Crisis Council. (1973). Charter. (Available from Crime Victims' Center of Chester County, Inc., P.O. Box 738, West Chester, PA 19381).

Reid, Wm. J., & Smith, A. D. (1981). Research in social work. New York: Columbia University Press.

Reimann, B. C. (1973). On the dimensions of bureaucratic structure: An empirical reappraisal. Administrative Science Quarterly, 18, 462-476.

Riger, S. (1984). Vehicles for empowerment: The case of feminist movement organizations. Prevention in Human Services, 3, 99-117.

Rothschild-Whitt, J. (1976). Conditions facilitating participatory-democratic organizations. Sociological Inquiry, 46, 75-86.

Rothschild-Whitt, J. (1979). The collectivist organization: An alternative to rational-bureaucratic models. American Sociological Review, 44, 509-527.

Rothschild, J., & Whitt, J. (1986). The cooperative workplace. Cambridge: Cambridge University Press.

Scully, R. (1983). The work-setting support groups: A means of preventing burnout. In B. Farber (Ed.), Stress and burnout in the human service professions (pp. 188-197).

Simon, B. (1981). The institutionalization of social movements: Rape as a case study. Unpublished Ph.D. dissertation, Bryn Mawr College, Bryn Mawr, PA.

Simon, B. (1982). In defense of institutionalization: A rape crisis center as a case study. Journal of Sociology & Social Welfare, 9, 485-502.

Singh, J., House, R., & Tucker, D. (1986). Organizational change and organizational mortality. Administrative Science Quarterly, 31, 587-611.

Solomon, B. (1981). Social work values and skills to empower women. In A. Weick & S. Vandiver (Eds.), Women, power, and change (pp. 206-214). Silver Springs, MD: NASW.

Sullivan, G. (1982). Cooptation of alternative services: The battered women's movement as a case study. Catalyst, 14, 39-57.

The Birth Center. (1978, August 28). Articles of incorporation. (Available from The Birth Center, 918 County Line Road, Bryn Mawr, PA 19010).

The Birth Center. (1981, January). Minutes of Board meeting. (Available from The Birth Center, 918 County Line Road, Bryn Mawr, PA 19010.

The Birth Center. (1988, April 18). Organizational chart of The Birth Center. (Available from The Birth Center, 918 County Line Road, Bryn Mawr, PA 19010).

The Birth Center. (1988). Director job description. (Available from The Birth Center, 918 County Line Road, Bryn Mawr, PA 19010).

The Crime Victims' Center of Chester County, Inc. (1977, July). Charter. (Available from Crime Victims' Center of Chester Couty, Inc., P.O. Box 738, West Chester, PA 19381.

The Crime Victims' Center of Chester County, Inc. (1987-1988). Annual report. (Available from Crime Victims' Center of Chester County, Inc., P.O. Box 738, West Chester, PA 19301).

The Feminist Therapy Collective. (1974, March). Articles of incorporation. (Available from the Women's Therapy Center, 1930 Chestnut Street, Philadelphia, PA 19106).

The Feminist Therapy Collective. (1977). Feminist therapy: A working definition. (Available from the Women's Therapy Center, 1930 Chestnut Street, Philadelphia, PA 19106).

The Feminist Therapy Collective. (1982, July 15). Report of the task force. (Available from the Women's Therapy Center, 1930 Chestnut Street, Philadelphia, PA 19106).

The Feminist Therapy Collective. (1984, November). FTC Constitution. (Available from the Women's Therapy Center, 1930 Chestnut Street, Philadelphia, PA 19106).

Thompson, J. D. (1966). Organizations in action. New York: McGraw-Hill.

Valentich, M., & Gripton, J. (1984). Ideological perspectives on the sexual assault of women. Social Service Review, 58, 448-461.

Victim Services Center of Montgomery County. (1988). '88 annual report. (Available from Victim Services Center, 527 Swede Street, Norristown, PA 19401).

Victim Services Center of Montgomery County. (1989, August). Agency history and services. (Available from Victim Services Center, 527 Swede Street, Norristown, PA 19401).

Weiner, M. (1982). Human services management: Analysis and applications. Homewood, ILL: Dorsey

Weisbord, M. (1976). Organizational diagnosis: Six places to look for trouble with or without a theory. Group & Organization Studies, 1(14), 430-447.

Weisbord, M. (1978). Organizational diagnosis: A workbook of theory and practice. Reading, MA: Addison-Wesley.

Women Against Rape. (Undated). Organizational goals and objectives. (Available from Delaware County Women Against Rape, P.O. Box 211, Media, PA 19063).

Women for Sobriety. (Undated). By-laws. (Available from Women for Sobriety, P.O. Box 618, Quakertown, PA 18951).

Women for Sobriety. (1976). The program booklet. (Available from Women for Sobriety, P.O. Box 618, Quakertown, PA 18951).

Women for Sobriety. (1988). WFS Motto. (Available from Women for Sobriety, P.O. Box 618, Quakertown, PA 18951).

Women In Transition. (1972, September 25). Articles of incorporation. (Available from Women In Transition, 125 South 9th Street, Philadelphia, PA 19107).

Women In Transition. (1982). A facilitator's guide to working with separated and divorced women. (Available from Women In Transition, 125 South 9th Street, Philadelphia, PA 19107).

Women In Transition. (1988, November 7). Women In Transition fact sheet. (Available from Women In Transition, 125 South 9th Street, Philadelphia, PA 19107).

Women Organized Against Rape. (1972). By-laws. (Available from WOAR, 125 South 9th Street, Suite 601, Philadelphia, PA 19107).

Women Organized Against Rape. (1976-77, Winter, Inaugural issue). WOARPATH. (Available from WOAR, 125 South 9th Street, Suite 601, Philadelphia, PA 19107).

Women Organized Against Rape. (1981). Power an empowerment. (Available from WOAR, 125 South 9th Street, Suite 601, Philadelphia, PA 19107).

Women Organized Against Rape. (1981). The work of Women Organized Against Rape. (Available from WOAR, 125 South 9th Street, Suite 601, Philadelphia, PA 19107).

Women Organized Against Rape. (1989). Background and history of Women Organized Against Rape. (Available from WOAR, 125 South 9th Street, Suite 601, Philadelphia, PA 19107).

Women Organized Against Rape. (1989, Summer). WOARPATH. (Available from WOAR, 125 South 9th Street, Suite 601, Philadelphia, PA 19107).

Women's Center of Eastern Montgomery County. (1975, November). Womenews. (Available from Women's Center of Montgomery County, The Benson East, Suite B-7, 100 Old York Rd., Jenkintown, PA 19046).

Women's Center of Eastern Montgomery County. (1976, June 13). By-laws. (Available from Women's Center of Montgomery County, The

Benson East, Suite B-7, 100 Old York Rd., Jenkintown, PA 19046).

Women's Center of Eastern Montgomery County. (1980, May 13). Minutes of Board meeting. (Available from Women's Center of Montgomery County, The Benson East, Suite B-7, 100 Old York Rd., Jenkintown, PA 19046).

Women's Center of Eastern Montgomery County. (1981, September 12). Minutes of Board meeting. (Available from Women's Center of Montgomery County, The Benson East, Suite B-7, 100 Old York Rd., Jenkintown, PA 19046).
1989, September). Womenews. (Available from Women's Center of Montgomery County, The Benson East, Suite B-7, 100 Old York Rd., Jenkintown, PA 19046).

Women's Center of Eastern Montgomery County. (Undated). Women's Center of Montgomery County brochure. (Available from Women's Center of Montgomery County, The Benson East, Suite B-7, 100 Old York Rd., Jenkintown, PA 19046).

Women's Resource Center. (1975). Women's Resource Center brochure. (Available from Women's Resource Center, P.O. Box 309, Wayne, PA 19087).

Women's Resource Center. (1989, September/October). Newsletter of Women's Resource Center. (Available from Women's Resource Center, P.O. Box 309, Wayne, PA 19087).

Women's Suburban Clinic. (1973). Articles of incorporation. (Available from Women's Suburban Clinic, East Paoli Medical Park, 1440 Russell Road Paoli, PA 19301).

Women's Suburban Clinic. (1973). Minutes of Board meeting. (Available from Women's Suburban Clinic, East Paoli Medical Park, 1440 Russell Road Paoli, PA 19301).

Women's Suburban Clinic. (1977, June 6). Minutes of Board meeting. (Available from Women's Suburban Clinic, East Paoli Medical Park, 1440 Russell Road Paoli, PA 19301).

Women's Suburban Clinic. (1989, January). Minutes of Board meeting. (Available from Women's Suburban Clinic, East Paoli Medical Park, 1440

Russell Road Paoli, PA 19301).

Women's Suburban Clinic. (1987). Philosophy Statement. (Available from Women's Suburban Clinic, East Paoli Medical Park, 1440 Russell Road Paoli, PA 19301).

Women's Suburban Clinic. (1989, July). Newsletter of Women's Suburban Clinic. (Available from Women's Suburban Clinic, East Paoli Medical Park, 1440 Russell Road Paoli, PA 19301).

Women's Suburban Clinic. (Undated). Counseling services. (Available from Women's Suburban Clinic, East Paoli Medical Park, 1440 Russell Road Paoli, PA 19301).

Zald, M. N., & Ash Garner, R. (1987). Social movement organizations: Growth, decay, and change. In M. N. Zald & J. D. McCarthy (Eds.), Social movement in an organizational society (pp. 121-142). New Brunswick, NJ: Transaction.

Index

Abortion clinic   59, 60, 61, 63, 75, 107, 113
AIDS/HIV   5, 62, 63, 101, 116
Alcoholic   88, 90, 97
Alcoholics Anonymous   52, 89
Alcoholic women's self help groups   54, 55, 89
Aldrich and Mueller   20, 21
Allied studies   135
Alternative organizational forms   3,1 0, 23, 26, 147, 148, 149
Alternative organizations   1, 2, 3, 4, 6, 9, 10, 16, 32,33, 34, 120, 123, 127, 131, 136, 146, 147
Alternative service organizations   120
American Association of University Women   72, 79
Archival documents   40
Authority   11
Authority structure   31, 32, 45, 111, 110, 137, 152
A Women's Place   37, 38, 39, 43, 44, 47, 48, 49, 50, 51, 111, 112, 116, 125, 126, 127, 128, 129, 134, 140, 143, 144, 145

Bailey, M.   67, 116, 121, 135, 137, 1420 141, 144, 157
Battered women's shelters   2, 12, 15, 20, 21, 22, 25, 34
Berkeley radical therapy model   104
Biordi, J.   106, 122, 130, 137, 142
Birth Center   48, 75, 76, 77, 78, 120, 121, 127, 128, 132, 134, 138
Black   3
Blackwell   5
Board of directors   53, 55, 63, 66, 70, 74, 75, 76, 81, 85, 86, 88, 90, 94, 97, 100, 118, 121, 131, 141, 146, 149, 150, 157
Board members   50, 51, 76, 105, 137
Brown, M.   92, 93
Bucks County feminist organizations   37, 43, 44
Budgets   135
Bureaucratization   16, 17, 18, 25
Bureaucratic organizations   1, 4, 5, 6, 10, 11, 12, 26, 31, 33, 147
Bureaucratic structures   16, 18, 21, 23, 33, 110, 133, 139, 141, 146, 147, 157
Burnout   155, 156
Byrne, D.   81, 82, 83, 116, 133, 145

Case study method   161
Center for Contextual Therapy   62, 135
Chambless, D.   104, 139
Change   6, 7, 15, 29
Cherniss and Krantz   153, 154, 160
Chester county feminist organizations   37, 43, 44
CHOICE   4, 38, 60

Circular relationship 142
Client service goals 29, 33, 111, 112, 116, 148, 152, 154
Co-directorship model 66, 73, 96, 98, 131
Collectives 16, 17, 18, 21, 23, 98, 103, 110, 120, 123, 133, 139, 152
Collectivist-democratic organizations 10, 11, 12, 31, 122
Collective structure 7, 12, 13, 33, 66, 95, 133, 138, 133, 137, 146, 152
Collins and Whalen 25
Committees 133
Comprehensive victims' services organization 86, 107
Conceptual model 29, 30
Conclusion of the study 162
Consciousness-raising group 56, 63, 68, 84, 95, 102, 111, 132, 149
Conservatism 16, 18, 19, 20, 21, 22, 25
Coordinating Office for Drug and Alcohol Abuse Programs 88, 89, 90, 92, 97, 114, 115, 119, 121, 122, 123
Crime Victim's Center of Chester County 37, 39, 43, 44, 48, 56, 57, 58, 113, 114, 123, 129, 134, 140
Current Managers of Feminist Organizations 145

Dale, J. 68 ,69, 71, 118, 123, 128, 129
Data Analysis 110
Data collection method 40, 41, 42
Davidson 1, 16, 17, 18, 19, 21, 23, 29, 33, 35, 122, 133, 137, 140, 142
Decentralized service model 161
Decision making process 15, 66, 80, 86, 94, 95, 98, 101, 103, 138, 139, 142, 157
Decision making structure 7, 14, 17, 24, 49, 152
Delaware County feminist organizations 37,44
Democratic organizational structure 14
Department of Public Welfare 87
Descriptive analysis 110, 142
Descriptive variables 29
Design 34
Difference between alternative
    feminist & traditional bureaucratic organizations 111, 161
Differentiation 11
Dimensions of organizations 7, 10, 111, 142, 147
    Division of Labor 111, 151, 152
    Formalization 111, 148, 149
    Goals 111, 147, 148, 161
    Organizational structure 111
    Personal relationships 111, 149, 150
    Rewards 111, 150, 151
    Six dimensions at two points of time 111, 142, 147, 161
    Year one & current year 111

Director   51, 52, 76, 141, 150
Division of labor   7, 11, 12, 31, 45, 130, 131, 151
Domestic Abuse Project   37, 39, 43, 44, 63, 65, 66, 67, 68, 111, 116, 117,119, 120, 124, 125, 129, 131, 132, 135, 136, 137, 140, 141, 142, 143, 144, 145, 149, 155, 157, 157, 148, 161
Domestic violence   48, 49, 80, 107, 132
Domestic Violence Center   39, 120
Domestic Violence Coalition   50
Domestic Violence Organization   112
Dormond, E.   78

Ecological theory   20
Egalitarian   13, 14, 17, 18, 24, 25, 33, 110
Elias, S.   128
Elizabeth Blackwell   4,38
Empowerment   155, 157, 159
Environment   20
Environmental factors   20, 22, 26, 29, 45
Environmental variables   20
Epstein, Russell, and Silvern   15, 29, 33, 35, 133, 137, 140, 142, 151
Executive director   125, 129, 140, 141, 145, 146
Exploratory study methodology   40
External communication   119

Fee-for-service   62, 98, 104
Feminist beliefs   3, 87
Feminist ideology   12, 15, 19, 21, 22, 24, 125, 139, 143
Feminist management   146, 155, 155, 157
Feminist movement organization   111, 139, 149
Feminist organizations   2, 3, 4, 5, 6, 12, 13, 14, 15, 16, 17, 18, 19, 21, 22, 23, 24, 25, 26, 27, 29, 33, 34, 35, 36, 47, 83, 84, 110, 111, 122, 123, 125, 133, 142, 143, 145, 146, 147, 149, 152, 153, 155, 160, 161
Feminist principles   2, 3, 5, 117, 137, 142, 143, 145, 147, 149, 157, 161
Feminist therapy   104, 123
Feminist Therapy Center   127
Feminist Therapy Collective   102, 103, 104, 105, 106, 119, 123, 126, 127, 131, 137, 138
Financial problems   127
Findings of research study   147, 152
First Funding Coalition   3
Formalization   14, 15, 29, 33, 42, 90, 111, 117, 120, 122, 148,150
Freeman and Hannan   19, 20
Feminist clinic   62,
Ferree & Hess   3
Founders   93, 129

Frantz, B.   43, 44, 47, 49, 50, 51, 127, 130, 141, 144
Funding sources   21, 25, 31, 32, 49, 51, 70, 98, 107, 136, 148
Future research   160, 161

Galper & Washburne   12, 22, 29, 34, 95, 109, 110, 131
Gilhool, C.   86
Girth and Mills   16
Goal displacement model   16, 113
Goal transformation   16, 17, 25, 113
Goals   6, 7, 9, 14, 17, 20, 21, 22, 24, 29, 42, 110, 111, 114, 115, 116, 142, 147, 148
Gordon   158
Grant writing   76, 126
Growth   27, 30
Gusz, M.   44, 56, 57, 58, 113, 123, 129
Gutierrez, L.   155

Hacker, R.   97, 98, 153
Hall   31, 32, 111, 130, 137
Helpful mechanisms   10
Hicks, W.   89, 90
Hierarchical structure   13, 33, 51, 61, 66, 70, 83, 86, 97, 139, 140, 152, 153
Hollos, S.   59, 60, 61, 62, 76, 77, 78, 111, 117, 121, 127, 128, 132, 139, 156
Hooyman and Cunningham   35, 117, 140, 148, 152
Hopkins, N.   72, 73, 112, 117
Hornstein, R.   90, 91
Hotline   99
Human service organizations   3, 4, 12, 13, 14, 155, 157
Humme, E.   64, 65, 66, 67, 119, 120, 121, 126, 127, 131

Ideology   24
Impersonality   123, 150
Implications   147, 153
Incentive structure   11
Information pamphlet/brochure   117, 120
Interim House   37, 38, 43, 44, 48, 88, 89, 90, 91, 92, 119, 120, 121, 122, 123, 134
Internal variables   23
Internal communication   119
Interorganizational relationships   22, 25, 32

Jackson and Morgan   119, 141
Job descriptions   117, 120, 149
Job sharing   12
Job specialization   33, 90, 135, 151

Job titles   131, 134, 135, 136
Johnson   12, 15, 21, 22, 29, 109
Junior League   60, 132
Justice Commission   64

Kalton   37
Katz & Kahn   15, 26, 33, 34, 126, 133, 137, 147, 150, 151, 152
Kimberley   35, 46, 47
Kirkpatrick, Jean   43, 44, 52, 53, 54, 55, 130, 137
Korean Women's Support Committee   82, 83, 115
Kulp, K.   101, 116, 133, 135, 136, 141, 142, 153, 160

Laurel House   81, 83
Leadership   9, 10, 13, 24, 27, 31, 32
Life cycle model   26
Longitudinal research   35

Management structure   103
Management training & skills   145
Marital Abuse Project   63, 64, 65, 68, 69, 120,1 21, 122, 127, 131
Material rewards   128, 130
McCarthy and Zald   15
McMahon, S.L.   95, 96, 97, 131, 137, 138
McShane & Oliver   2, 12, 13, 14, 15, 21, 22, 29, 31, 32, 110
Methodology   40
Michels   16, 113
Midwifery   77, 78
Mikols, P.   103, 104, 123, 131
Montgomery county feminist organizations   37, 39, 43, 44
Murray   25, 34

National Coalition Against Domestic Violence   65
National Organization for Women   56
Naturalistic design   34
Network of Victims Assoc.   39
Newman   1, 17, 18, 19, 21, 23, 29, 32, 33, 34, 123, 124, 127, 133, 136, 140,
      142, 151
New Life   52
New You   55
Newcomers   94
Newsletters   118
Non-experimental research design   34, 35
Non-hierarchical   10, 14
Non-probability purposive sample   35, 36

OASIS program   97, 98
Oligarchization   16, 17, 18, 20, 25
OPTIONS for Women, Inc.   4, 38
Organization   9, 10, 12, 13, 15, 16, 17, 18, 19, 20, 21, 22, 24, 25, 26, 29, 31, 32,
    35, 41, 111, 115, 116, 117, 118, 123, 124, 125, 126, 128, 135, 136, 138, 141,
Organizational change   21, 41, 147
Organizational chart   55, 117
Organizational development   3, 9, 15, 16, 19, 26, 161
Organizational diagnosis   9
Organizational dimensions   6, 9, 19, 26
Organizational forms   5, 9, 14, 19, 20, 21, 23, 26, 27
Organizational goals   111, 113, 119
Organizational growth   31, 32
Organizational leaders   145
Organization's life cycle   15, 47
Organizational structure   119
Organizational theorists   33, 147
Organizational transformation   17, 18, 142
Organization stage of development   41, 42, 46, 161

Paid staff   57, 74, 82, 87, 89,94, 98, 100, 124, 126, 128, 130, 134, 135, 137,
    146, 150 ,153, 160
Part-time   61,90,106,128,134
Pennings   40
Pennsylvania Coalition against Rape   57, 70, 87, 102, 112, 160
Pennsylvania Coalition Against Domestic Violence   65, 81, 82, 96, 98, 112, 156
Perlmutter, F.   1, 12, 13, 14, 15, 24, 33
Personal Relationships   7,10,31,42,111,122,123,149,151
Philadelphia County feminist organizations   36, 43, 44, 97
Philadelphia Health Management Corp.   90, 91, 92
Philadelphia Women's Network   37, 43, 44, 48, 87, 92, 93, 94, 95, 115, 122,
    127, 129, 134, 136
Pigford, N.   93, 94, 95, 129
Pilot case   10
Pilot study   6, 7, 26, 29, 31, 32, 33, 110, 111
Pines and Aronson   153, 154, 155
Pinto, J.   99, 132
Pines and Aronson   155
Planned Parenthood   60, 132
Political activities/advocacy   61, 62, 153
Powell   1, 112, 120
Price   40
Procedures manual   117, 120, 149
Professionalism   23, 86, 88, 137, 150
Population ecology theory   9, 19, 26, 34

Powell   120
Problem drinking   53
Pro-choice rallies   117
Pugh   31, 117
Purpose   9, 12
Purposeful rewards   130, 150

Qualitative methodology   40

Racial composition   90
Radical ideology   19
Rape   70, 107, 113
Rape crisis centers   2, 5, 17, 25, 57, 111, 116, 160
Rape Crisis Council of Chester County   56, 58, 88, 113
Rape Crisis Council of Montco   85, 86
Rape crisis movement   25
Rape Crisis of California   50
Rape Crisis Organization   112
Rape victims   69, 70, 84, 86, 99, 107, 112, 123
Recruitment and advancement   11
Reid and Smith   34, 35, 40
Relationships   9, 13
Reproductive rights   78
Research questions   33, 34
Rewards   12, 13, 15, 45, 126, 150
Reward system   9, 31, 111, 150
Riccio, K.   84, 85, 86, 113
Riger, S.   2, 3, 12, 13, 14, 15, 21, 23, 24, 29, 31, 32, 33, 110, 111, 113, 114, 122, 139, 142, 149
Right-to-Life movement   61, 63
Roe vs. Wade   59, 61
Rothschild & Witt   1, 6, 10, 11, 12, 31, 110, 112, 113, 119, 122, 123, 126, 127, 130, 132, 137, 138
Rules   11, 152

Salaries   129
Sampling   35
Sample selection   36
Sayre, B.   81, 132, 151
Schwartz, A.   5
Scully   154
Senior Safety Project   64, 65, 69
Simon   118
Singh, House and Tucker   19, 35, 41
Simon, B.   15, 17, 18, 19, 22, 23, 24, 25, 32, 33, 35, 113, 118, 123, 142

Sliding scale fee   106
Specialization   77, 90, 135, 136, 152
Social change   2, 3, 24, 33
Social change goals   12, 14, 24, 29, 111, 112, 116, 117, 147, 148, 152
Social control   11
Social movement organizations   15, 16, 17, 18, 19, 20, 35, 161
Social relations   11
Social service agencies   21, 22
Social service goals   12, 14, 24, 110
Social stratification   11
Staas, S.   71, 72, 73, 74, 75, 125, 128, 135, 158
Staff meetings   144, 155
Staff meeting minutes   117
Structure   9, 12, 17, 20
Structured interview   41, 43
Sullivan   1, 2, 12, 15, 21, 22, 29, 32
Support groups   52, 53, 54, 71, 95, 149, 154
Supreme Court   63

Take over   90
Task Force   119, 139
Theoretical model   15, 27
Therapists   104, 105
Thompson   15
Times out   155
Traditional bureaucracies   13
Traditional human service organizations   3, 4, 5, 6, 12, 14, 22, 26, 32
Traditional organization   1, 4, 9, 12, 32, 33
Traditional authority structure   110
Transformation of feminist organizations   21
Transactional relationships   26, 27
The Birth Center   37, 39, 43, 44, 75, 76, 78, 107, 120, 127, 139

United Way   37, 51, 58, 73, 75, 80, 82, 85, 87, 90, 97, 98, 106, 107, 137

Valentich & Gripton   13, 24, 25, 31, 110, 111
Valuing of Process   144
Victim and Witness Assistance Services of Chester County   48, 56
Victim Services Center   37, 39, 43, 44, 84, 86, 87, 88, 108, 113, 114, 134, 140
Volunteers   7, 49, 57, 58, 64, 65, 66, 67, 70, 71, 72, 73, 74, 77, 79, 81, 82, 83,
    84, 85, 87, 100, 123, 124, 126, 128, 129, 130, 150, 151, 153, 160
Volunteer Empowerment Council   66

Walters, G.   88, 89, 123
Weber, B.   51, 113, 128, 130, 145, 146

Weber-Michels Model   16, 17, 18, 19, 22, 23, 25, 113, 119, 148, 149
Weiner   113
Weisbord, M.   9, 10, 29, 112, 117,130
Whitt   1, 6, 10, 11, 12
Women's Action Coalition   63, 64, 68, 69, 71, 123, 127
Women's Advocacy Project   84
Woman Against Abuse   38, 116, 120
Women Against Rape   39, 43, 44, 48, 64, 68, 69, 70, 71, 87, 111, 112, 113, 118, 120, 123, 128, 129, 134
Women for Sobriety   37, 39, 43, 44, 48, 52, 53, 54, 55, 126, 122, 127, 130, 134, 135, 144
Women in Transition   37, 38, 43, 44, 48, 63, 68, 95, 96, 97, 98, 103, 111, 115, 117, 118, 122, 125, 131, 134, 138, 139, 145, 156, 157, 158
Women Organized Against Rape (WOAR)   4, 38, 44, 48, 56, 68, 69, 98, 99, 100, 101, 102, 111, 116, 117, 118, 122, 123, 128, 129, 132, 133, 134, 135, 137, 141, 144, 153, 156, 157, 160, 161
Women's Alliance for Job Equity   38
Women's Association for Women's Alternatives   39
Women's Center   2,71,79,81,82,134,136,148
Women's Center of Montco   37, 39, 43, 44, 48, 79, 80, 83, 87,1 13,117,118,119,126,129,134,136,140,147,160
Women's Law Center   38
Women's Law Project   4, 38
Women's Liberation Center   95
Women's movement   2, 3, 17
Women's Resource Center   37, 39, 43, 44, 48, 71, 72, 73, 74, 111, 112, 115, 118, 124, 125, 128, 129, 134, 135, 139, 157
Women's Suburban Clinic   37, 39, 43, 44, 48, 59, 60, 61, 62, 63, 75, 76, 78, 79, 111, 117, 120, 121, 127, 128, 129, 132, 133, 134, 135, 141, 143, 144, 156
Women's Therapy Center   37, 38, 43, 44, 48, 102, 105, 106, 111, 119, 122, 126, 128, 130, 142
Women's Way   3, 4, 37, 67, 90, 97, 98
Worker-collective organization   17
Written meeting minutes   118, 119

Zald & Ash Garner   14, 15, 16, 19, 20, 23, 26, 33, 126, 147, 148